A HISTORY OF LADAKH

A HISTORY OF LADAKH

A. H. FRANCKE

GYAN

Published by

Gyan Publishing House
5, Ansari Road
Daryaganj, New Delhi-110002
Phone: 011-47034999, 9811692060
E-mail: books@gyanbooks.com

Distribution Network
gyanbooks.com
India, USA, Canada, UK, Australia

ISBN: 978-93-7133-784-7 (PB)

First Published, 1904

2nd Impression 2025

Printed at: Gyan Press, Delhi.

A HISTORY OF LADAKH
Author: A. H. FRANCKE

A HISTORY OF LADAKH

A History of Ladakh

A.H. FRANCKE
with
CRITICAL INTRODUCTION AND ANNOTATIONS
by
S.S. GERGAN & F.M. HASSNAIN

STERLING PUBLISHERS PVT LTD.
NEW DELHI-110016

A History of Ladakh
by A.H. Francke
Critical Introduction and Annotations by S.S. Gergan & F.M Hassnain
(Published originally as *A History of Western Tibet* by A.H. Francke)

Published by S. K. Ghai, Managing Director, Sterling Publishers Pvt Ltd.,
AB/9 Safdarjang Enclave, New Delhi-110016.
Printed at Sterling Printers, L-11 Green Park Extn., New Delhi-110016

Author's Preface

It is now a little over fifty years since General Sir Alexander Cunningham wrote the first outline of Western Tibetan history. It is found in his *Ladak*. Since then a great mass of material which is of historical interest has accumulated, and thus the time has arrived for the compilation of another popular history of that country. I do not say, "for a scientific history." That may be written when all the historical records of whose existence we know have been edited. There are such historical records, which it is extremely difficult for a European to get hold of, although there can be no doubt about their existence. Among them are the chronicles of several lines of vassal-princes. But, as the principal historical work, the *Ladvags rgyal rabs*, the "Book of the Kings of Ladakh," has been translated in a masterly manner by Dr Karl Marx, late Moravian missionary at Leh, we may now venture on a popular history of Western Tibet, without running the risk of making gross mistakes. Still, there can be no doubt that in another fifty years it will be possible to write a still more reliable book on the same topic. I am particularly glad that this history gives me an opportunity to place before a larger public the results of Dr Karl Marx's excellent historical studies, and thus to give expression to my gratitude to my beloved teacher.

As some knowledge of Buddhism is nowadays considered to form part of one's general education, I have not thought it necessary to explain every one of the many Buddhist mythological names occurring in the book. Only those which are of a purely local interest to Ladakh have been explained.

My thanks are due to Dr F. E. Shawe, of Leh, for kindly reading the first rough copy of my MS., and for many suggestions, additions, and corrections, with regard to the subject-matter; to Major F. M. Peacock, the well-known military noveli st for many suggestions with regard to improving the style; and to the Rev. C. J. Klesel, Secretary of Moravian Missions, for kindly attending to the final revision.

The Tibetan names are spelt in a way to make them pronounceable for English readers. All the vowels should be pronounced as in German or Italian.

A. H. FRANCKE

CONTENTS

LIST OF ILLUSTRATIONS

(facing page 64)

MAPS

Critical Introduction

LADAKH HAS been termed as Western Tibet by Western writers and the Greater Tibet by oriental scholars. It has fascinated many a traveller from far off lands since ancient times. Fa-Hian and Ou-Kong seem to have visited Ladakh in the fourth century. Mirza Hyder Dughlat, who invaded Ladakh in 1534, has given a vivid description of its topography. The Jesuit missionaries who reached Leh in 1631 have described it in their travel accounts. The other writers in the field were: William Moorcroft, Hederson, Torrens, Ujifarvy, Hedin and Crump. Most of them have provided us with their travels and adventures in Ladakh. Alexander Cunningham and Fredric Drew have given us a lucid account of their geographical surveys in Ladakh. As regards the history of the region, we have a standard book available by A.H. Francke entitled *History of Western Tibet*, which has been selected by us for critical appreciation. We have tried to rectify important issues so as to complete the work of Francke and have avoided minor issues because these do not adversely affect the main narration of historical events.

Since the publication of the book in 1907, a systematic search for historical documents in the form of manuscripts, charters or *Ka-shog*, treaties, stories-treatises and diaries maintained by various people was conducted by Revd. J. Gergan and others in Kashmir, Spiti, Zanskar, Lahul, Bushahar (Khunu). As far as possible, the original, were collected, in whatever condition they may be. Copies of the eulogy recorded on tempora for the laying of foundation or consecration and dedication of a

Stupa were carefully made. Special mention needs to be made about one of the oldest Stupas at Sani, Zanskar, known as Kanika-Chhod-tren (Kanisk's Stupa). A eulogy is inscribed on the stucco surface of the wall of the Assembly Hall, in the middle of which the Stupa containing the relics of the Buddha is preserved, and also a short description on the life of the Buddha. The author states that this Stupa is one of the eight most important Stupas of the Buddhist world—De-ched (b Debyed) at Magadha, Gu-u-Don (Gu-U-Don) at Singhala; Cha-run-kha-shor (Bya-run-kha-shor) at Nepal; Ge-u-Don (Gu-U-don) at Senge-ling; Go-Ma-Sa-A-Gandha (Go-ma-sa-la-gandh) at Li-yul (Country of the Turks) now known as Sin-Kiang; De-chen-zho-nui-chhod-rten (bDe-chen-zho-nui) me-hod-rten at Za-Hor (Za-Hor), a town in Bengal; San-We-Gan-Dho-La (gSan-wai-gan-dho-la) at Udhyana or the present Swat etc.; Kanika-Chhod-Tren of Zanskar (Kashmir).

This eulogy includes a short description of important Buddhist towns and places in the valley. It is significant to point out, the author says, that actually Kashmir is the name of a town where Naropa (or Naropada) was born. Later, this name was applied to the whole valley.

Francke admits that there are several historical records of whose existence he is not aware. There are other historical records which are extremely difficult of access by a European, although there can be no doubt about their existence. Rev. Joseph Gergan collected a variety of historical documents in original, and where this was not possible, he had copies made. Out of these, a good portion was made available to Francke for his "History of Western Tibet", "Antiquities of Indian Tibet", and the other papers, which he published or retained unpublished.

In his introduction on page 5 he states: "In no case do the Western Tibetan chronicles enable us to fix the time of the reign of a king exactly. This clearly reveals that his chronology is defective. We have to point out that invariably in all Tibetan documents, charters, letters, receipts, dates are given in the Customary Tibetan Calendar, the Rab-jun. It needs careful calculation to obtain a date corresponding to the Gregorian, *Samvat* or *Hijra* era. To solve this important problem, a comparative chart had to be prepared, since the first introduction of Rab-jun into Tibetan usage and with the Gregorian era in 607 A.D.

The historical dates of kings, the date of birth, ascension to the throne, tenure of rule could very easily and with fair accuracy be fixed, with the help of the Charters, certificates issued by a king, king and queen, and sometimes the Crown Prince. The word of praise and eulogy written on the occasion of laying the foundation of a *Gonpa* or a Stupa, or a Mandang (generally known as *mani* wall) the praise to the king, queen, crown prince and other princes and princesses, the Chief Minister or *Ka-lon*, the Cabinet Minister, the head of the town or village or a district right down to the nearest relative and the workers (mason, carpenter, smiths, painter, calligraphist)—are recorded so that they may reap the reward of merit and are saved from the cycle of births. To gain merit, the names of the people who donate silver, gold, grain, butter, etc., and their services also are recorded. As such, Francke was not able to fix the dates of one of the famous Kings of Ladakh, Singe Namgyal, while the famous artist and the calligraphist has with accuracy recorded the date in colophon.

For invasion of Ladakh by the Dogras, Francke has drawn on the accounts given by Basti Ram, a Dogra senior officer under Zorawar Singh. After the death of Zorawar on 12 December 1841 he left Taklakot fort, "fires burning and horse tired", and alongwith 250 soldiers escaped over the Lepu-Lhas-pass into Almorah district. While crossing the high passes in snow and sub-zero temperature, most of his forces died and the rest of them were rescued by the Raja of Rajkot. The story recorded by Basti Ram is biased; it is but natural, especially when he wrote the story for Cunningham, a British representative, who was in the making of the northern frontier of British India! The vandalism perpetrated by the Dogra army is very vividly given in the diary maintained by the Private Secretary of the last three kings of Ladakh and also the story written by a retired Lama hermit hiding in a cave in the mountains of Lower Ladakh[1] (Sham).

1. Gergan S.S., *Ladags rGyalrabs Chimed Ster*, pp. 509-579.

Both the writers describe in detail how Zorawar Singh and his men carried off gold, silver, precious stones, silk, tea etc., emptying out the treasures of Ladakh palaces, *Gonpas* and temples of Tashigang, Chhumurti, Spiti, Thsale-rang, Tholing, Purang etc. They even removed the sacradotal utensils of silver, gold, copper, carpets, and silk and sent 70 ponyloads to Jammu. At Toyo, before Zorawar Singh's death, he calculated to have sent plunder totalling to the tune of 170 ponyloads of gold, silver, silk, carpets, tea (Lhasa) etc., and cash of Rs 37,000 in silver and gold to his master.

Barbaric vandalism committed by Dewan Hari Chand and Wazir Ratun and their soldiers surpassed Chengiz Khan. They looted all the *Gonpas* and temples, denuded all silver, gold and copper statues, and religious utensils except the Hemis Gonpa. They pulled down the palaces, mansions of Ministers and gentries, the monasteries, the University buildings and out of these materials they constructed forts, barracks for the army and quarters for the civil officers, and offices. For roofing, in place of birch bark they used the parchment paper written in letters of gold, silver and copper, the Scripture of the Buddha and birch bark imprinted with sacred Buddhist formulae.

The hermit Lama writes:

> "Once, where the Lamas used to congregate in the Lamayuru assembly hall, and used to recite the hymns to the holy Buddha, therein, mules, donkeys and horses are tethered and they bray from the windows. In the inner sanctuary, where the Abbot used to lead the congregation in prayers, horses are stalled. The sacred books have been destroyed and the rest are dumped in a corner like straw for the animals."

These documents have been reproduced in original in Gergan's *Ladags rGyalrabs Chimed Ster*. As Francke has totally missed these authentic documents, his account of the Dogra war on Ladakh cannot be considered as correct.

CHAPTER 1

Francke is correct in stating that the present population of

Western Tibet is the result of a long process of blending of at least three distinct peoples, two of which are of Aryan stock, whilst one, which is numerically superior to the other two, is of Mongolian origin. The Aryan nations are—the Dards of Gilgit and the Mons of North India, perhaps from Kashmir, but the Mongolians are of the Tibetan stock.

Gold is found in the alluvial flats of high level valley and the plateau of Changthang, the famous being the Thog Jalung gold fields; gold is also found in the sandy banks of the Indus and its tributaries right from Saspola to Chilas on Dardi Stan. The Ladakhi kings used to get from Guge 2186.25 gms. and from Rudok 1918.10 gms. of gold as annual revenue. This gold was used mostly for religious purposes—for gold plating of copper plates used for Stupas and icons of the Buddha, the Maitriya, the goddess Tara, Guru Padma Sambhava, Patron Lama of Hemis—Skushog Stagthsang Raspa, painting of scrolls or *Thankas* and books—the Kanjur and Tanjur and other books. Many such books were sent by the King of Na-ris-skor-sum and Ladakh to Lhasa, Tashi-Lhunpo and Bhutan to gain merit and release from the bondage of the "Wheel of Life". As today, this yellow metal became the bone of contention because the "Great Fifth", the Dalai Lama, very much wanted to acquire the rich gold field of Na-ris-skor-sum for himself. He appointed Galden Thsewang, a son of Dalai Khungteji, as a military commander and sent him together with the Mongol and the Tibetan troops against Ladakh. At that time, Galden Thsewang was acting as the Chief Lama Officer, who enforced discipline in the Tashi Lhunpo monastery in the absence of the Panchen Lama but Galden Thsewang failed to conquer Ladakh. Having failed to acquire Ladakh by military force, the then Dalai Lama very cleverly appealed to the Incarnate Lama of Bhutan, of the Ningma Dugpa sect, Mipham Namgyal to mediate between the Ladakh King and Sogpo Galden Thsewang. Mipham Namgyal did not play a fair game as he was under the influence of the Dalai Lama. The Prime Minister and his cabinet, who kept the Mongols at bay for three long years, succumbed to the religious importunity of Raj-Guru of Ladakh. The Ladakhi King had to hand over the area east of Lhari stream—Demchog to Sde-pa-Zhun (Lhasa) except the village of Menser, situated near the Kailash and Manasarovar.

In Ladakhi, Balti and Dardi folklore or in mythology, there is no mention of the famous gold digging ants. It is not understood how the Greek and the Roman authors got these stories! It is true that the Dardis, the Baltis and the Ladakhis obtain gold dust by washing the sand obtained from river banks or pits excavated on the banks of the Indus and its tributaries, right from Saspola to Chilas. The people had to pay a certain percentage of their land revenue or tax in the form of gold dust and other commodities or cash. Regarding the remarks on colour and purity of the Indus gold and the European gold, both appear ignorant as the Western Tibet gold is pale-yellow in colour and contains certain small impurity of silver, while the European gold ornaments are reddish yellow, and contain certain percentage of copper or alloy, to stand wear and tear.

Ptolemy mentions the nation of the Byltae which is the present Balti, or Persianized Balti-Stan, and there is no doubt about the location and the people, or the Thubbati-Khurd (little Tibet) of Muslim traders and geographers. We do not agree with the scholar's conjecture of assumptions like "Dabase" with dBus (Zan) or Ue of the Central Tibet. A careful study of geographical division reveals that Central Tibet or the Lhasa is situated at a distance of about 2,000 miles from the place. Ptolemy must have collected verbal information about these mountain-locked republics.[2] The distance from Mayum-la to Kyi-rong is 350 miles and this area is known as Stod. Kyi-rong to Shigatse is about 350 miles and this area is known as Tsang; Shigatse to Lhasa about 125 miles and this area is known as Ue or written as dBus. Literally dBus means the middle, the centre. It is particularly the name given to the Central Province of Tibet, wherein Lhasa the capital is situated.

Francke's indentification of the nation of "Dabasae" of Ptolemy with the Tibetan word of *dBus* is very far-fetched. When Ptolemy, the famous mathematician, astronomer and

2. The distance between Taxila and Lhasa is 2,067 miles : Taxila to Gilgit 250 miles; Gilgit to Skardo 165 miles; Skardo to Leh 214 miles; Leh to Demchok 210 miles: Demchok to Mayum-la 400 miles and this region is known as Naris-skor-sum.

geographer of Alexandra lived in the second century A.D., a unified Tibetan kingdom did not exist, but was divided into eight major lineages or tribes and sub-tribes or, independent republic states. It was only in the seventh century that Srong-tsan Sgampo unified these tribes into a powerful Tibetan kingdom and chose centrally and strategically situated Lhasa as the capital of Tibet. This province was designated as dBus or Ue or the "Centre". This dBus has no relation with Dabasae. Now the question arises: who were the nations of the "Dabasae" of Ptolemy? In our opinion, they were the people inhabiting the valleys that lie on the south side of the Hindu-Kush and the Swat valley or Gandhara, now known as Kafiristan, peopled by the Black and the Red Kafirs The name Kafir is a post-Islamic name indicating one who conceals the religion of truth or Islam and is an infidel. In ancient or pre-Islamic times, certain indigenous ethnic stock of this area were called Das-yus by the neighbouring countries. Now the Dardic-or the Shina-speaking people and the Pushto-speaking people use *Da-yus* as a word of abuse, meaning evil minded, mischievous, etc. It appears that the Arabic word 'Kafir' is an exact translation of, or rendering of, Das-Yus, or Da-Yus or Da-Oos.[3]

No further comments need to be added to Francke's remarks. Actually the question of Western Himalayan (Tibet) dialects—Balti, Purig and Ladakhi—needs a lengthy and exhaustive essay. Francke writes about the Mons: "In almost every Western Tibet village we find one or several families who are called Mon. Those people are mostly musicians or carpenters and are treated with little respect by the rest of the population. Their low position makes us to believe that they belong to a nation, originally different from the Tibetans, who were conquered in former days. But to find out who the Mons really were is impossible in most parts of Ladakh...."

Francke emphatically affirms that it is impossible to find out who the Mons really were, but he is certain on one point: that the Mons belonged to an Aryan race, who lived in the

3. *Das-yus* meaning slaves or enemies (*A Brief History of the Indian People* by Sir W.W. Hunter.)

Indus valley before the Dardis or the Tibetans conquered and occupied the country, but he has not been able to prove as to who the Mons were!

In the Tibetan dictionaries the word 'Mon' is defined as the general name for different nations and *tribe* as Kiratai,[4] and Hindus in general, living between Tibet and the Indian plains such as Nepal, Paldo in Bhutan, Assam and Kulu, and who from remote antiquity have lived by hunting. Their physical characters are definitely Aryan; long or medium head, face narrow, nose prominent and narrow; well formed nose bridge, cheek bones not prominent as the Mongolian; eyes well-formed and right angled to nose; fair or wheat-coloured and dark-skinned; hair dark and soft; beard fully developed, body medium or tall. The physical characters have remained almost purely Aryan to this day, and this is due to their stigma of belonging originally to a low class or caste of a subject race.

All over the ancient kingdom of Zun-Zan, now the vast area enclosed by the Ma-Yum-la in the East, Udhyana-Swat-Gilgit in the West, Pamirs in the North and Spiti, Lahul, Zanskar in the South, Mon graves (Mon-dur), Stupas (Mon-gyi-Chhod-rten), Mon-castle (Mon-mKhar), Mon-fields (Mon-Zhin) are found, but so far no written documents have been discovered except the "Ye Dharma" formula, in ancient Indian characters.

The only source by which the origin of Mon race could be traced now is their language. Gergan has made a detailed study to trace the lineage of the Mons by philology, but it is not the scope of this introduction to record in detail. Here it is enough to record that the Mons are not of Kashmiri descent, but belonged to a different race. Mons call a Kashmiri *Kyir* or *Kir*, people of Tibet and Kham are called *Zun-Zan,* Baltis are called *Tu-ruk*, Mons called themselves *Manus* or *Desi-si-manus*, or the inhabitants of the country or aboriginal.

The Mons have made a specific distinction between the Kashmiri and themselves. Had the Mons been of Kashmir

4. *Kiratai* means one who constantly walks on the extreme boundaries. The ancient Aryans, familiar with the term, mention the *Kirrhada* who used to bring musk from the Himalaya for sale to Indians. (Sarat Chandra.)

stock and descent, or branched off from the same stem or race, they would never append the contemptuous name of *Kirah*[5] or *Kir-mlechchas* to their own forefathers, the Kashmiris.

Imposing remains of ancient Buddhist art are found all over north and north-west India, right from Leh to Bamian, and also ancient Tibetan and Brahmi or Gupta scripts.[6] These works of art in stone, and inscriptions were executed by the people of the upper Indus valley and not the Kashmiris. Kashmiris would have preferred to write the caption, eulogy or the dedication in *Sharda* script instead of *Brahmi*, Gupta or Tibetan.

It is enough to record that the *Mons* were not of Kashmiri descent but belonged to one of the ancient Aryan races who were pushed into the higher valleys and Indus valley by the waves of Aryan races and other peoples who migrated into the Indo-Gangetic plains. Francke bases the migration of the Dardis on three main points and draws his conclusions:

1. The present territory of areas where Dardi is spoken;
2. Dardi colonies according to the *Hymnal* of *Bonono* festival; and
3. Dardi colonies according to archaeological remains.

On the first point, the occupation by the Dardis in the Dras valley and Dah-Hanu in the Indus areas need no comment. As for the Dardi colonies on the Indus, alleged to have been established by the Dardiṣ according to the *Bonono Hymnal*, differ from Francke. He appears to have jumped to the conclusion about the establishment of the Dard colonies without accurately ascertaining the creation of each hamlet and village as recorded in the *Hymnal*. It appears that he was not able to locate the exact geographical position of Ron-chhurgyud with the help of Survey maps as he admits "...all the villages mentioned in the songs are well known places. If they cannot

5. A. Cunningham, *Ancient Geography of India* pp. 92-93. That the Baltis are not Tibetans or Mongols but descendants of Sacae or Scythians (by Herodotus) is proved by scientific data collected by the renowned anthropologist Ch. de Ujtalvy (1920).
6. *Man and Past and Present* (1920), p. 164.

be found on maps, it is due to the terrible orthography of Indian maps." (p. 102.) It is obvious that he did not visit or tour the areas of Balti Ron-chhu-rgyud, otherwise he would not have made the gross mistake of replacing Lower Rong-chhu-rgyud by the Upper Rong-chhu-rgyud, which is separated by a distance of 260 miles or about 400 kilometres. There are two Rong-chhu-rgyud or gorges in the district of Ladakh (pre-partition or pre-1947), one in the Leh Tehsil and the other in Skardo Tehsil. The upper Rong-chhu-rgyud is the narrow Indus gorge, lying between Nyidar and Martselang in Leh Tehsil. The lower Rong-chhu-rgyud is the deep, perpendicular rocky gorge between the wide Indus valley of Skardo and Stag village on the Indus. Stag is the last village where Balti or Tibetan is spoken. All the villages and hamlets mentioned in the *Bonono Hymnal* are now indicated in the Survey map, and are geographical entities, between Sathsil and Hanu villages.

From the perusal of the *Hymnals*, it is more than clear that the emigrants found a suitable site for settlement for themselves and their flock of goats and sheep, suitable cultivable areas for field crops and fruits very similar to their original Dardi home Sathsil, which they left behind. There is no mention in the *Hymnal* that the land they adopted was inadequate or insufficient but there is praise for the vast verdant pastures and fertile land.

During the course of centuries, there might have been migration of stray individuals or families but no bulk migration of a tribe to the Upper Indus valley, beyond Hanu and Khalatse, is indicated.

In Chapter IV on pages 39-40, Francke has remarked: "It was believed for sometime that one of the earliest of them, Fa-Hian, say 400 A.D. had passed through our country, because the description he gives of the kingdom of Kie-Cha in his diary *might actually pass* for a description of Ladakh. Therefore, A. Cunningham accepted Kie-Cha as the Chinese rendering of some ancient name of Ladakh; and Legg identified Kie-Cha with Skardo in Baltistan. Modern scholars, in particular A. Stein, have proved, however, that Kie-Cha stands for Kashgar in Turkistan."

We have to differ from all the above scholars on the

identification of Kie-Cha with Ladakh, Skardo, and Kashgar in Turkistan.

As in more than half a dozen references by ancient and modern Chinese historians, the Chinese name for Kashgar is Hru-Ie-Lie in Sin-Kiang and *not* Kie-Cha. In *Pilgrimage of Fa-Hian* p. 25, Note 3, Sou-Le or Hru-i-li is identified with Kashgar and not Ku-Cha or Kie-Cha. A calculation of the duration and direction of Fa-Hian's journey, and the description of the road, flora and fauna, hazards of passes, mountains and desert etc., and the Chinese rendering of Kie-Cha, reveal that the place is Kashgar of the Chitral valley and not the Kashgar in Turkistan.

It is proved and admitted that Buddhism was carried to Eastern Turkistan, Central Asia and China by the Buddhist missionaries from Ariana (Taxila), Gandhara and Kashmir etc. Fa-Hian and other Chinese Buddhist Bhiksu students, to acquire first-hand knowledge and education, must have selected the then best Buddhist Seminary or University on the recommendation of their teachers, Chinese or non-Chinese, deputed from these Universities. The documents discovered from Takla Makan and Tun-Huang by Aurel Stein prove fairly conclusively that their authors were Tibetan, Chinese, Indian and Mongols.

Before proceeding from their homeland, China, the pilgrims must have taken into consideration the long and tedious journey through waterless deserts, and arid mountains, glaciers and bandit-infested areas, and must have chalked out their programme very carefully about—

1. Their subsistence—the Buddhist *Bikhsus* are bound by their vows to maintain themselves only on the alms doled out by not less than three lay-givers (sBin-bDag). As such, perforce they had to accompany a big caravan, the members of whom were obliged to dole out alms for the feeding of the Bhikshus.

2. Due to changed geographical conditions, dessication of these areas, sand and loess burying cultivated land, orchards, towns and monasteries, Fa-Hian and his caravan must have chosen a regular highway or trade route like the famous Silk Route. From the description recorded by Fa-Hian in his diary, it is obvious that he took the direct trade route to Gandhara

from Khotan, Kokiayar over the Tsongling mountains, the Pamirs and the famous Darkot pass down into the Kashgar valley (Chitral).

3. Fa-Hian must have taken the shortest route between Khotan and the sacred places where the relics of the Buddha were preserved, such as skullbone, tooth, staff, mantle, pot, or where he performed miracles—feeding a ravenous tiger with his own head—Taxa-Shila (Taxila) and Gandhara, Peshawar, Swat. From his diary it is obvious that he took the right direction and the shortest distance from Khotan to the above places and not through Kashmir.

4. Fa-Hian never had Kashmir on the list of places which he wished to visit. He could have very easily visited from Swat, Dardistan and Taxila, as there was a regular traffic in a Buddhist country, where he could have all the facilities as a Bhikshu pilgrim coming from far distant Maha-Chin.

It is enough to say that Fa-Hian never visited Kashmir or passed through Kashmir to see the sacred places in the Arya Desh, the home of the Buddha. On page 42, Francke has asserted "During the time of the Chinese progress in the far West, Turkistan, Western Tibet and Kashmir became part of the Celestial empire. The conquest took place during the first part of the eighth century.[7]

History of Tibet (629-896 A.D.) written recently by the Chinese historian Fhan-win-lan in Chinese, translated into Tibetan by a team of scholars at Dharamsala, states that in 644 A.D. Srontsan Sgampo conquered Zan-Zun and there were several rebellions by the people of Zan-Zun to regain their independence, but they were finally subdued by Thi-srong-Ide-tsan (754-707 A.D.). He subdued Sumbha, Tu-goo-Zan-Zun and Sin-jan. Latest research by Chinese historians does not,

7. In no Tibetan literature, tradition or geography is "A Man of Maryul" called a Marpa. A Marpa is an inhabitant of Lhobra in Central Tibet to both tribes or the clan and the Place or the valley is called Mar and Mar-Pa as the famous Tibetan scholar Mar-Pa Dopa Chhos-Kyi-Wan-Chhug of Yar-Dog, resident of Mar-Do. The word Mar-yul is derived from a clan, tribe or lineal name of Rma + Yul country or the country of the Rma people. For further details please consult *Ladags rGyalrabs* by Gergan, pp. 627-628.

however, support the above statement; as such Western Tibet never became a part of the Chinese empire. The sending of the first embassy might have been only an Eastern custom of goodwill and courtesy, not of subjugation. One must make a note here what the Chinese religious teacher Confucius had stated: "There are no two suns in the sky; no two kings in a land; and no two princes in a State and no two Chiefs in a family." The Chinese assumed that other kings were barbarians and could not be granted the status of equality, and their Emperor was the Emperor of the entire world. If Kalhana makes no mention of the Chinese assertion he appears to be correct, as the king of Kashmir must have sent presents and not tribute ! It may be pointed out here that the Chinese were never able to conquer Baltistan, but their object was to halt the Baltis and the Tibetans on the left bank of the Indus and the Gilgit rivers, to prevent them from crossing over to the right bank and control the West Gate—Darkot. The Chinese wanted to keep the Darkot Pass, the Western Gate which controls Oxus, Kunar, (Chitral), Gilgit, the Pamirs, the Sin-Kiang valleys and the main Indus valley. In 678 A.D. when the Chinese were not able to face the combined forces of Tibetans and Baltis, they attacked the Tibetans in Eastern Tibet near Thso-Snon. When the Tibetans were hard pressed they had to divert some force and officers to Eastern Tibet (p. 402.) The Chinese were able to capture Darkot Pass, chased the Tibetans down to the junction of the Gilgit river to the Indus. The Chinese did not dare cross over to the left Bank of the Indus, Baltistan, but they destroyed the suspension bridge to stop further attack by the Tibetans (pp. 174, 175). As such, the assertions made by Francke on page 44 are not correct.

Of particular interest to us is that the Chinese annals speak of "Great and Little Poliu"; from this we infer the names of "Great and Little Tibet". This name is found in the works of the later Kashmiri historians.

The inference arrived at by Francke in ascribing "Great and Little Poliu" for Great and Little Tibet, e.g., for Tibet proper and Baltistan is *not* correct. Chinese call the Greater Tibet or Tibet proper Thu-u-Fhan and the Tibetans Shie-Jan and not "Great Poliu". For Baltistan they have adopted phonetically the Dardi name for Baltistan Po-Lo-Lo, since the Chinese tongue found no difficulty in pronouncing it, as the name is devoid of the letter "R". All the Chinese pilgrims and explorers refer to Baltistan as Po-Lo-Lo. In no documents have the Chinese used Poliu for Baltistan. The "Great Poliu" and "Little Poliu" are the two provinces or valleys of Yasin and Kunar or Beilam river in which Chitral is situated.

The two adjectives "little" and "great" are the distinguishing adjectives appended to Tibet by Arab traders. The Nestorian Christians and Arab traders first came in contact with the Tibetan speaking Sbalti or Balti, later they came in contact with Tibetan-speaking people mostly on the south of the Silk route, who were called *Tubet* by the Mongols. The Arabs called them *Tubbet*; they found Eastern Tibet a vast kingdom stretching from Sin-Kiang to the border of China, so they added "Great" to Tibet and "Little" to Sbalti, converted into Greater and Little Tibet. The Arab traders who traversed from Spain to India must have transmitted these names, Great and Little Tubbet, to Europe. Marco Polo uses the form Te-bet and devotes two chapters to its description. It is a grave mistake to confuse 'Poliu' with 'Po-Lo-Lo' as in Chinese, change of a vowel sound, or even a stress on a syllable or tone makes considerable difference in meaning. In our opinion, both Great and Little Poliu are situated on the right bank of the Indus, below the big bend or knee. To us Great Poliu is the Chilas area and Little Poliu comprises the countries situated on the Gilgit river—Yasin Gilgit area etc. It tallies with and is proved from the description given by Fa-Hian about this area.

Darad-speaking people of Daradistan-Gilgit area and the Darads inhabited the neighbourhood of Baltistan and Dras-Shimsha Kharbu down to Suru river. The Baltis are known as 'Po-Lo-Lo' in Shrin language, and while speaking Tibetan they refer to themselves as Sbalti. The Baltis themselves and all Tibetan-speaking people, right from the borders of China to Kargil, call the people Sbal-Ti, and the country Sbalti-Yul, and have recorded these names in the most ancient records and the modern languages.

The progress of the Chinese in the far West was conducted on the north side of Kunlun mountains into the Tarim basin.

But they did not dare to disturb the hornets nest—the Tibetan plateau, where the Tibetans wielded supreme power. As already discussed above, the Chinese wanted to take possession of the strategic passes of the Pamirs. They never attacked Baltistan or Po-Lo-Lo, but they cut off the approach and passage of the Tibetans via Po-Lo-Lo and Great and Little Poliu. It must be made clear here that the Chinese never ruled over Ladakh Maryul, Naris-skor-sum or Zan-Zun, but maintained good relations by exchange of presents and letters through representatives.[8] Francke's assumption that Kashmir became a part of the Chinese empire during the eighth century is not true. There are clear references to Chandrapida and Muktapida in the annals of the T'ang dynasty. They sent their ambassadors to the Chinese court to seek help against the advancing Arabs towards the north west of India. The description of the valley given in these annals have been copied from the records of earlier pilgrims to Kashmir It was Lalitaditya who learned superior military techniques from Central Asia and China and imported experienced soldiers also. It is in this context that he obtained the services of Chunkuna, a Tokharian from the Tarim basin, who had earlier served the Chinese.[9]

Lalitaditya was a great conqueror and his conquests included some parts of central Asia also. He also defeated the Tibetans and these victories were celebrated not only during his life time, but even long after.[10] His aim was to obtain the support of the Chinese against the Tibetans and in this connection, he offered to encamp the Chinese forces on the shores of the Wular lake in Kashmir. But nothing came out of this offer, for the Chinese empire itself was in the process of disintegration due to internal and external troubles. Similarly, Francke's assumption that Kashmir paid and continued to pay tributes to China is totally incorrect.

Cessation of political relation between China and the northern

8. Gergan S.S., *Ladags rGyalrabs*, pp. 455-459. However, several battles were fought between China and Central Tibet and there was a change of hands for the Tibetan-speaking areas in the Kun-lun region etc., but not in Ladakh or Naris-skor-sum areas.
9. *Archives of Asian Art, XXVIII*, 1974-75, p. 32.
10. Kalhana, *Rajatarangini* (trans. Stein), IV, pp. 168-308.

kingdom of India was due to the rise of Tibetan power in the east and also to the rise of Islamic power and pressure from the west. Another contributing factor was the emergence of Uigur and Mongol powers on the north western borders of China. To preserve his way of life—highly civilised, luxurious and sophisticated—the Emperor, and the peace-loving aristocracy escaped from occasional waves of attack by the Mongols, Tartars and the Tibetans hordes by moving their Capital Kaifeng in the north to Hanchow on the sea-coast in the south. On page 44, Francke has remarked that in the north there is a road which penetrates into Poliu or Baltistan; in addition to our earlier discussion of Poliu we need point out that Srinagar-Bandipur-Gurais-Burzil Pass road is known as the Gilgit Road and not Skardo road. From very ancient times, this road was the link between the Kashmir valley and Dardistan, the Great Poliu-Yasin and the Gilgit valley and Little Poliu—Chitral in the Kashgar valley. There was regular traffic between all the Dardia-speaking areas, right from Gurais, Astor, Bunji, to Gilgit, Yasin, Ashkoman or to the watershed of the Pamirs for 8 to 9 months till the Burzil and Tragbal passes became impassable due to heavy snow. There is no doubt, that there is a summer by-pass road over the Burzil Pass to Skardo over uninhabited mosquito-infested Deosai plateau, where there is no shelter old or new, no fuel, animal transport, rations, and one has to depend on ones own resources. The weather is erratic, alternated by hail storm, rain, freezing cold and burning sun. The regular highway to Baltistan is via Zojila, Kargil to Skardo.

In Chapter V, on page 47, Francke has remarked, "As we have shown in the previous chapters the irrigable valleys of Western Tibet had been brought under cultivation by the Aryan tribes of the Mons and the Darads, and the latter especially exhibited an extraordinary skill in the construction of water courses along almost inaccessible cliffs."

Before going into details of the alleged engineering skills of the Darads, we would like to go into the derivation of the Tibetan word for Darad. In Tibetan a Darad is called a Dogpa and they call themselves Shin or Shrin. The literal meaning of *hDog* is wilderness, uncultivated land, summer Alpine pasture land, *Yalaq* or *Behk* for cattle, horses, flock of goat and sheep—*hDogpa* is synonymous with herdsman, shepherd, or people who live in tents, or nomads in moorland, upland valleys or plateaus tending cattle, sheep, ponies etc., subsisting on the produce of livestock such as butter, cheese, mutton, beef, wool, hides, etc. In Tibetan *Dogpa* is a general name given to all nomads, irrespective of their nationality, language, class or creed, the people of Chongthang who depend only on livestock and who do not possess houses, but live in tents are called *Dogpa.* Had these Shrin people been agriculturists by profession, the Tibetans would not call Dardi Shrin as Dogpa. The Shrin or the Darads who migrated from Dardistan and settled in the Indus valley mainly depended on dairy or animal husbandry and farm products, the Tibetans must have denominated by their professional and occupational name without any reference of bias to their race, blood, religion or rational affinity to the indigenous Mons. The *Hymnal* of Dardic migration very clearly indicates that they were of pastoral habit, and depended less on agriculture. The engineering skill in chanellizing water from mountain streams or springs by means of an aqueduct, *Kuhl* or *Kol* along almost inaccessible cliffs is the skill of *Sbalti* or Balti, who is a born engineer, his engineering skill being sought all over the Ladakh district. He has an inborn instinct for alignment, his 'eye' will act as the most accurate levelling instrument, would lead without any difficulty an aqueduct or channel along most precipitous rocky cliffs by building in dry rubble stone masonry cemented by ordinary clay and mud. Almost all the water channels in the Dardic village of Dah-Hanu etc., is the work of skilled Balti and not the indolent Dard. The *Dards* and the Changpa Dogpa of Changhang are known for their indifferent ways and unhygienic habits. These characteristics stem from their occupation. One or two men, women, boys and girls with a couple of mastiffs or sheep dogs can easily take care of flock of two to three thousand sheep and goats. The yak and ponies do not need any herding, they are let loose to graze, they are not stall-fed. Attacks of wolves or wild dogs or some leopard are warded off with ease with blank gunfire. The rest of the family members spin wool or hair of goats and yak for their tents and tweed, the rest while away their time in drinking tea, Chhang and dicing or gambling.

This is not so with an agriculturist, who cannot afford to be lazy, in fact the entire family has to work hard from spring to late autumn or face starvation. In winter they are busy tending the farm animals and spinning and weaving coarse tweed for the family.

The Dogpas settled down as husbandmen, but cattle or the flocks of sheep and goat mainly form their chief wealth. They have no separate word for wealth ("Nor"), sheep and goats being termed "Nor" (wealth). A rich or wealthy man is called Nor-Chan, also a man possessing many goats and sheep, etc. The Gujars and Bakerwals also call cattle "Mal", a rich man is known as "Mal-dar", that is, owning many heads of cattle. All these nomads have to pay or accept dowry or fine in currency of heads of goat or cattle, indicating their original occupation. It also reminds us of the Latin word for money Pecunia, from pecus, a herd, the same as Ladakhi "Chhugs".

On page 79 Francke has remarked that the lively barter between the tribes apparently led to many matrimonial bargains as well, and so a race grew up which combined in itself the agriculturist and the nomad. Francke again remarks, "From local tradition and inscription it is possible to gather some scanty information about the various states which were in existence before the time of the Central Tibetan Dynasty. At Leh there reigned a dynasty of kings who derived their origin from the mythical king Kesar; "Alchi Khargog". It is true there existed some very important and celebrated tribes of Tibetan stock in the Indus valley between Ma-Yum-La (the watersheet of the Indus and Brahmaputra) and Dardic country. In the ancient Tibetan records this area was known as Zan-Zun, which included Purang, Guge, Rudok, Chhumurti, Spiti, Gar-za or Lahul, Zanskar, Maryul, Ladakh, Sbalti, and Gilgit.[11] Even uptil now the above areas are Tibetan-speaking areas with the exception of Gilgit. The Muslim historians have mentioned a Tibetan prince ruling in the Kabul area.[12] Curiously, the Sbalti speak one of the most ancient forms of Tibetan, pronouncing the prefixes and the superscribed consonants

11. Gergan S.S., op. cit. (*vide* pp. 184-188, *Ladags Rgyalrabs*.
12. *ibid.*

alike in Khams which borders on China. In both localities the same minor irregularities occur, transgressions against an exact rendering of the pronunciation according to the letters.

Zan-Zun is the name of a tribe or lineage. Out of the eighteen main Tibetan lineage or tribes Zan-Zun and Rma or Smra seem to have moved *en masse* from their original home in Central Asia or the watershed of the rivers Yangtse Kiang and Hwang Ho and occupied the upper Indus valley and valleys of the tributaries, the Sutlej and the Chenab, unoccupied by the aboriginal Mons, and formed into small independent republic States. They did not intrude into the other areas or the valleys of the Indus and the Shayok inhabited by the Sbalti. In due course of time the lineage or the tribal name was adopted —Zan-Zun and Smra-Yul, later corrupted to Mar-Yul. Traditionally, this could be correct, and it is possible that a branch or sub-tribe to which rGyalpo Kesar belonged might have migrated along with Zan-Zun and Rma or Smra (as there are some families in Ladakh who still, on certain occasions, worship the same deity as that of Kesar) and settled in the Indus valley. The main tribe must have remained in their ancestral home in Kham, as king, Ling-Tshang alleged to be the direct descendant of Kesar, with more than fifty families, including his own, fled from Kham in 1952-65 and took refuge in India. They are now settled in the Tibetan colony in Dehra Dun. With the intermixing of the Mons, Tibetans, the Sbalti and the Dogpa or the Dards over the centuries, their common faith—Shamanism or Bonism, later Buddhism—and other common denominators like food-habits, dress etc. enabled them to give up their nomadic ways and acquire stability as a settled people. Thus a new community came into being.

Chronology

There is a wide difference in the chronology given by Francke in his work and the actual dates provided by the authentic documents and manuscripts, some of which have been reproduced in his monumental work on the history of Ladakh by Gergan. The following comparative statement in respect of important dates may be useful :

Name of the king	*Francke's Date*	*Correct Date*
Sengge Namgyal	*c.* 1590-1620	1569-1594
Deldan Namgyal	*c.* 1620-1640	1594-1659/60
Delegs Namgyal	*c.* 1640-1680	1660-1685
Nima Namgyal	*c.* 1680-1720.	1685-1720
Deskyong Namgyal	*c.* 1720-1740	1720-1739
Puntsog Namgyal	*c.* 1740-1760	1739-1752
Tshewang Namgyal II	*c.* 1760-1780	1752-1782
Tshetan Namgyal	*c.* 1780-1790	1782-1808
Tshespal Namgyal	*c.* 1790-1841	1808-1830
Tshewang Rabrtan/ Chhog Sprul	?	1830-1835
Nurub Stanzin (Installed by Zorawar Singh)		1835-1839
Jigmed Chhos-ki-Senge	—do—	*circa* May 1840-1842
Magna Thanadra (first Governor of Ladakh)		1841-1845.

Francke has not given any details about the invasion of Ladakh by Sultan Zain-ul-abidin of Kashmir. After having secured the allegiance of the Baltistani chief, the Sultan invaded Guge and later reached as far as Shay.[13] Here he saved the golden image of Buddha from destruction at the hands of soldiers, and returned to Mulbe which can be identified with the present Mulbek as indicated in the map.[14]

Chapter VIII

Francke states "The population of Baltistan, as well as that of the rest of Western Tibet consist of Aryan and Tibetan elements; but as has been supposed by several writers, in Baltistan the Dard element is somewhat stronger than in other parts of the country, and this may account for certain superiorities in the character of the Baltis." Unsubstantiated conjectures made by Francke and others cannot be accepted as authentic. We are aware how the Tibetans are classified into known ethnic groups. They have classified known humanity into five major

13. Jonaraja, *Rajatarangini*, stanzas 833-834.
14. *ibid.*, st. 835.

races—(1) Chinese, (2) Mongols, (3) Iranians, (4) Indians, and (5) Tibetans. The Sbalti (Balti) as a sub-race have not been included in the Tibetan race but have been grouped under the Iranian ethnic group in spite of the fact that they speak Tibetan, and they had a Tibetan literary tradition before they adopted Islam as their religion.

The Sbalti is classified as a sub-ethnic group under 'Iranian'; the sub-groups are—Iranians, Taziks, Turks, Uigurs, Dards, Sbalti and two other sub-Turko Iranian groups. It may be noted that Sbalti is the only group who speak Tibetan. The oldest Chinese historians record that nothing could be said with certainty about the origin of the Tibetan race as it is shrouded in antiquity, but a people known as Shan-Sbi-Ee under the overall command of Thu-U-Li-Lo-O-Kui-Bu-Hun-Ni occupied the whole of the headwaters of Yangtse-Kiang and Hwang-Ho.[15] In 4-5 century B.C. hordes of Tibetan-speaking people left Tangut (or Tanghut), their native country, and advanced gradually by stages towards Zungaria in the West. During the course of their temporary stay, they appear to have mixed racially with the cattle-racing Central Asian tribes of the Mongols and the Turks and adopted milk and milk products like butter and cheese as articles of food. Here they had been settled for decades when invasion by a new horde compelled them to leave their adopted home and to migrate beyond the Pamirs to safer areas, e.g., the valleys of the Oxus and the Indus. The entire Tibetan-speaking people seem to have chosen the Indus valley and those of its tributaries, the Shayok, Shigar etc., guarded by the Mustagh massif in the north and the inhospitable, swampy, mosquito-infested, uninhabited Deosai plateau. The entire tribe—men, women, children—and their possessions of the bovine animals like yaks, cows, sheep, and ponies for transport or sport (polo), seem to have moved to their new home, in which they have been destined to live to this day.

As early as the second century A.D. Ptolemy described them as nomadic, living in woods and caves. The tribes of the Sakai, along the Jaxarte, are the Karatai and Komarai, and the people who are scattered over the mountain region are Komadai; those

15. *Gya-Yig-Tasang-Nan-gSal-Be Bod-Kyi rGyalrabs*, Dharamsala.

along the range of Askatangha are the Messagetai; the Crynsei or Skathai and Tooranai inhabit the intervening areas below which, along Mount Imaos, are the Baltoe.

The early geographers—Ptolemy, Ibn-Batuta, Abie-Rihan,—and Kashmiri, Tibetan and Chinese historians and travellers like Fa Hian, Huen-Tsang, all confirm that Baltistan or Little Tibet or the Sbalti-Yul of the Sbalti was inhabited by a Tibetan-speaking tribe classed under the generic designation of the Turks, and the Tibetans. The last of the Turks—Turks or Tibetan-speaking community—appears to have reigned in north-western India about 850 A.D., much before the first Tibetan king of Ladags—Mar-yul or Zan-Zun—Skid-lde-Nima-Gon, came from Central Tibet with one hundred horsemen and occupied Purang in 922 A.D.

It is interesting to note that the indigenous people of the Indus valley before the Tibetan occupation, the Mons, called the Sbalties by their generic name "Tu-Ruk" or Posal. The Mons make specific distinction among races or lineage and tribal groups. Inhabitants of Ladakh, Tibet and Kham are all Tibetan-speaking but in Mon-skad, the Ladakhis and Tibetans are called Manu and the Baltis, Turuk; the Kham people are called Zun-Zan or Zun. The Kashmiris are called Kyir or Kir.

Francke further writes : "The last we heard of the Baltis was their brave resistance against the Chinese conqueror in the eighth century". Regarding this, we may point out that the resistance against the Chinese was put up by the Tibetans who held the sway in Central Asia, and not the Balties.[16]

On page 108 Francke remarks : "The Baltis were the first Western Tibetans who became Mussalmans. Although we have no definite record to go by, Cunningham makes it probable that the change of religion took place some time about 1400."

On this point Mohibbul Hassan in his *Kashmir under the Sultans* remarks : "Shamsu'd-Din therefore left Kashmir with fifty of his followers and went to Baltistan where he continued his missionary activities and succeeded in converting many of its Buddhist inhabitants to his creed (Tuh fatul Ahbab). He remained for two months until the defeat and death of Sayed Muhammed

16. Thun-Che, *References from Chinese History*, pp. 162-63.

in 1505. It is obvious that Islam of Nurbakhshiya sect was introduced into Sbalti-Yul in 1505 A.D. Even now in Baltistan and Kargil in all the villages, right from Shakar-Chigtan (Tehsil Kargil) to the border of Gilgit both Nurbakhshiya and Shia sects are found."

Francke further remarks: "...the religion of the Baltis was a Tibetan form of Buddhism and the Tibetan alphabet was at least partly known. Besides this, the Baltis pride themselves also on having an ancient alphabet running from right to left".

The religion of the Balties was Mahayanic Buddhism and not a form of Tibetan Lamaism. The Tibetan alphabet, the U-chan, or with the head, was fully known to them, and they used it freely in rock inscriptions. (This is amply explained in the photograph below.) The Tibetan script or the letters are of archaic type as the vowel "i" is written in reverse direction.

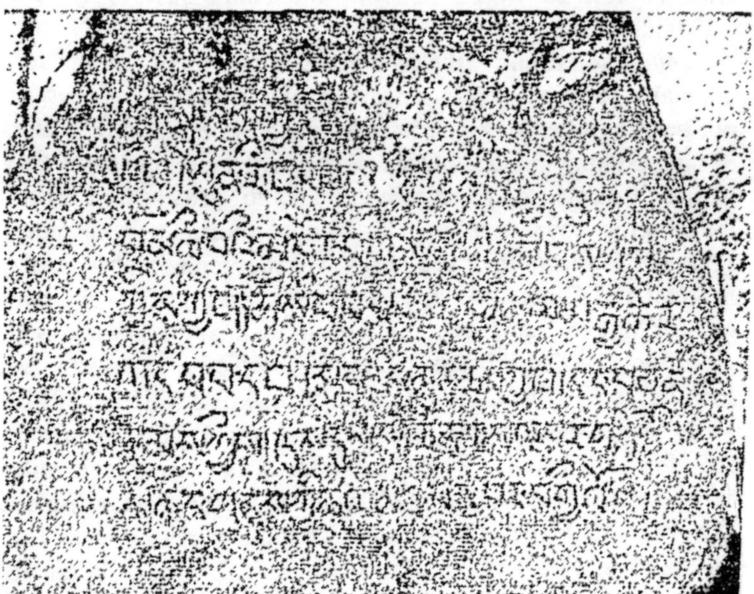

Francke states "The Balties apparently never had a king over themselves...they had *Magspons* or Dukes instead." About rulers or kingship, the Baltis are not exceptional in having Magspon or dukes or chiefs. In the whole of Zan-Zun which comprised the Indus valley alongwith its tributaries, right from Ma-Yum-La, the water-parting of the Indus and Brahmaputra to the borders of Dardistan and Gandhara, there were no kings, but there were small independent republics. It is only after Skid-Ide-Nima-Gon *circa* 922 A.D. that Naris-skor-sum had a king or kings. The ancient Cho or dukes were not deposed, but were given the former status etc., in respect of their position, holdings etc., but they had to accept the suzerainty of the King of Naris-skor-sum, Mar-yul, Ladakh, Spiti, Zanskar, etc.

Cunningham and Francke both are incorrect in stating that "the most important and probably most ancient Magspon family was that of Khapulu..."

The present "Cho" family of Khapulu is known as the Yab-Go family and they do not belong to the Mag-Spon family, and they have not descended from any royal family. Their ancestry can be traced back to the community of Saddle-makers.

Yab-go in archaic Tibetan literally and actually means saddle-maker, perhaps saddler or cart-wright. The Yab-go family do not belong to the Magspon lineage which is essentially a class of high-ranking military officers. Under the circumstances they had to fabricate their pedigree in books to prove that they belong to the royal family. This is not unusual as pretenders generally fabricate their pedigree. We may point out here that in Tibet and Central Asia, a profession does not make a man low or high in rank or status but individual quality and *Rus-pa* or blood. The Tibetan saying "If you like to kill a Chinese, then kill his bullock, and if you like to kill a Tibetan, kill his horse" here seems to be apt. A horse and a good saddle are the life of a Tibetan. A master craftman like a saddler is much in demand and is as respected as religious or secular leaders. It appears that when the Sbalti of Khapulu migrated from Tangut, and settled permanently in the Shayok valley, in the absence of a Duke or tribal Chief they must have elected the master-saddler or the Yab-go as their leader or Sarpanch. In the course of more than two thousand years, the descendants must have adopted the title Cho like other Cho in the area and fabricated the pedigree of descent from Alexander the Great.

INVASION OF MIRZA HYDER DUGHLAT : 1532

Francke has given no information about the invasion of Ladakh by Mirza Hyder Dughlat in 1532. In his *Tarikh-i-Rashidi*, the Mirza writes as under :

> "When I reached Nubra, I invited the people to accept Islam and a great number, among them submitted. But the nobles and their chief did not submit and fortified themselves. In a siege all these were routed and most of them were killed or captured. After this defeat no one dared to oppose me. Then I marched with my soldiers towards Leh and its two rulers waited upon me and offered there submission. After some time, after consulting my advisers, I decided to attack the valley of Kashmir."[17]

Jamyang Namgyal, circa 1560-1590: The above two dates are not correct, as Jamyang Namgyal died in 1569 A.D. This is confirmed by Stag-Tshan-Raspa, the first Sku-Shog of Hemis, in his biography. The succession to the throne by Senge Namgyal and his coronation in 1569 A.D. and his death in 1594 A.D. are all recorded in Stag-thsan's biography; and also confirmed by Namkha-Spalgon calligraphist's eulogy and colophon recorded in a aRgyad-Ston-Pa. This correction in date is very important as there is a wide difference between Francke's dates and Gergan's dates as all the later dates are dependent on the death of King Senge Namgyal. Francke has not definitely located Urgyan or Udyana of Tibetan Ujjana of Pali and Uchan-na or U-chang of Chinese is Swat and its neighbourhood of the present day. Udyana would thus have embraced the four modern districts of Panjkora, Bijawar, Swat,

17. Mirza Hyder Dughlat, *Tarikh-i-Rashidi*, trans. p. 417.

and Bunir, which have a circuit of only 500 miles if measured on the map direct, but not less than 800 miles by road measurement. Fa Hian mentions Su-Ho-To as a small district to the South of Udyana. This has generally been identified with Swat. Darel was the ancient capital of Udyana or Urgyan. The celebrated Padma Sambhava is much connected with Udyana, and the Nyingmapa sect in Ladakh is intimately connected with Udyana.

Deldan Namgyal, circa 1620-1640: Deldan was crowned in 1596 at the demise of his father, Senge Namgyal, and ruled for 63 or 64 years (1659/1660). The above dates are confirmed by Muslim historians also.

CHAPTER IX : THE GREAT MONGOL WAR, ABOUT 1646-1647

Cause of Mongol War: (1) The Great Fifth, Ngawang Lobzang Gythso, the Dalai Lama (1617-1682), through his religious authority, made his influence felt in the political affairs of Mongolia and among the Buddhist Chinese and Tibetan-speaking people in China. He tried to exert his influence over the Buddhists of countries neighbouring Tibet—Bhutan (aDrug), Sikkim (aDras-Ljons), Nepal (Bal-bo), and Ladakh (Bla-Dags) in order to extend the sway of the Lhasas and Gelugpa or Reformed sect. The people of Bhutan, Sikkim, Nepal and Ladakh belong to various Nin-ma-pa or the Ancient or Unreformed Red-hat sects as Ka-Gyupa, Jonangpa, Karma-pa, Degungpa etc., and they are vastly different from the Gelugpa or Reformed sect. These differences in persuasion, often lead to acute tension, several times culminating in hostility and armed clashes, between the Gelugpa and Ningmapa sects. In Ladakh, the majority of the Gonpas and the people being of the Ningmapa sect, and the Patron Lama of the Ladakh king since Jamyang .Namgyal being Stag-Thsang-Raspa-Ningmapa of Dugpa sect, and the tutelary Guru (teacher) being Guru Padma Sambhava, the Ladakh kings Deldan Namgyal and Senge Namgyal and the Church did not pay much heed to the persuasion by Lhasa. Even Senge Namgyal drove out the Mongol invaders from Naris-skor-sum, and raided some villages of

of Ee-gu, Chem-re, Tang-Tse and Tashi-gang etc., however, did not cooperate with the Mongols, and the latter had to advance towards Lower Ladakh. Fierce battles were fought, the enemies army had to retreat to Bazgo, where they laid siege to Basgo Castle for six months. They used catapults to destroy the castle and the temple of Chamba, but were not successful. In the meantime Ka-lon Shakya Gyathso went to Kashmir to seek the assistance of Emperor Aurang Zeb-Alam Gir. In Shin-Pho-Chi-Lo 1684 A.D. a huge army left Kashmir under the command of Nawab Fidai-Khan, Gori Khan, Lashkar Khan, Gakha Sultan, Yah-i-Yah Khan and Jahan Gir Khan. They spanned four bridges at Khalatse in their onward march. A fierce battle was fought at Thang-skya Thang-nag, and the Mughal army routed the combined Mongol-Tibetan army who fled and entrenched themselves in the Leh palace. The Turko-Mughal army stormed Spituk village where the Tibetans and Mongols (Sogpo) were hiding, and soon captured the Mongols and Tibetans and also the local people whom they could not distinguish from the former. The Mughal army wanted to storm Leh palace and to capture the Tibetans and the Mongols. King Jamgyang Namgyal intervened and requested the Mughal officers to save his palace. The Sogpo (Mongol) and Tibetans fled to Tashigang from where they witnessed the end of their short-lived glory. Aurangzeb's forces returned to Kashmir with the crown prince Jig-Dal-rNamgyal as a hostage.

SECOND INVASION : 1684

In the Shin-mo-lan (wood-female-ox year), 1684-85 A.D., the Tibetan and the Mongols came back and burnt Le-Palace. History repeated itself and more than 6000-7000 Mughal soldiers descended on Leh. A fiery battle was fought at Abi-Chhen-Mo-Thang, on the out-skirt of Le town. The Tibetans were defeated and fled again to Tashi-Gang; they built a moat and fortifications round the castle and bided their time for an opportunity to come back to Leh for negotiations. When Sde-pa Zhun (Lhasa) was convinced that Ladakh could not be subdued by force, they tried to make inroads through the finer sentiments of religion!

The Great Fifth (Dalai Lama) and the Cabinet Ministers well knew the people of Ladakh whose kings were staunch Ningmapa, and also knew their psychology. So they very cleverly approached Dugpa Mi-Pham-Wan-Po, the Pontiff of the Ladakh king, to mediate for peace and subtly arranged to acquire the rich Naris-skor-sum area. Sdepa-Zhun appealed to the Pontiff of Ladakh kingdom, stretching from Ma-yum-la to Baltistan, subjugated by the Muslim (Mlechh) king of Delhi, and attempted to persuade him that sooner or later the whole of Ladakh would be converted to Islam, as such Ladakh should be saved from the Muslim influence. The Pontiff was granted a huge estate in Tibet in lieu of services rendered to the Dalai Lama, besides an extraordinary reception given to him when he visited Tibet! Ka-lon Shakya Gyathso and his Cabinet, who were considered wise and experienced persons, faithful to the king and fatherland, succumbed to the gentle, courteous, and sly arguments of Dugpa Mipham Wangpo. Delegs Namgyal had to submit to the decision of his Raj-Guru the pontiff; in the literal sense, the King and his Cabinet were fascinated by the magnetism of the Lama, agreed to hand over the richest province consisting of three districts of Guge, Purang, and Rudok to Lhasa, and to exchange triennial presents or Lo-chhag with Lhasa. This treaty of 1684/85 established the Ladakh and Tibet border at Demchhok, Spangyur etc., and has remained in effect to this day.

To promote the Ge-lugs-pa sect Prince Nawang Namgyal (Delegs' son) was sent to Lhasa under duress and indoctrinated and trained as a Gelugs-pa priest. On the completion of his seminary training, he obtained the degree of Shes-Nen-Rab-Jams. Before returning home the Dalai Lama conferred on him a certificate written on golden yellow China silk over 20 cubit in length (30 ft.) To consolidate the supremacy of the Gelugpa sect Nag-wan-phun-thsog, son of Sogpo Ghaldan Tshewang, was appointed as the Khanpo of Thiksay gonpa, and other gonpas of Ningmapa sect. He was also asked to build a "Debating Hall" on the lines of that of the Geldanpa sect. The above measure were taken to convert Ningmapa sects to Gelugpa sect, or the Red cap to Yellow cap. The Khanpo wisely did not exert any pressure on the Ningmapa sect or his supremacy followed the principle of "live and let live". Honouring the Lhasa ecclesiastical order in letter, he constructed a room or an assembly hall (Du-khan) but not a regular "Debating Hall". The translation of an official letter in Mongolian script addressed to the Khanpo is reproduced below :

Ga-ldan Tshering-dWang-po sends this letter to the Khanpo of Khri-rtse.

> "Your letter sent by way of Turfan (Turman) was very pleasing to me. It was very nice to hear of your zeal regarding the teaching of Tson-ka-pa, and your belief in Tsong-ka-pa's teaching which is founded on that of Manjusri (aJam-dPal). Tsong-ka-pa. We are pleased to hear that dPal-ldan Shesrab, the nephew of Stod-Shes-rab bZangpo has introduced everything according to the rule or canon, and the clergy will show their zeal. As a token of present, we are sending a piece of red foreign cloth."

The letter written in 1694 A.D. was addressed to Nono Lo-Zan-Nag-Wan Phunthsog, Khan-Po and Geshe.

Stag-Tshang Raspa did not sit tight, but in order to disseminate the teachings of Guru Padma Sambhava evolved and instituted a festival in summer in order to commemorate the birth of Guru Padma-Jun-Nas, popularly known as Hemis Tshes-chu or the Hemis festival. He also instituted "Theg-Chhog Gi Wan-Chhog", the great initiation of the Mahayana.

CHAPTER X

Nima Namgyal : Francke places Nima Namgyal's reign between 1680 and 1720 A.D., but actually he ruled from 1685 to 1720 A.D. Francke has dealt very briefly with the reign of Nima Namgyal; in spite of his much reduced dominion, he resumed active diplomatic contacts with almost all the surrounding neighbouring countries—China, Tibet, India and Russia. It appears that he made up for the reduced kingdom by active trade and diplomatic facilities. He believed in democracy, so he vested more powers in the Panchayat and virtually they took all the important decisions. His worthy image was tarnished by the jealous Muslim concubine when the question of succession was decided upon. Already the small kingdom was divided into two; Purig, Zanskar and Spiti were given to Tashi Namgyal, the rest was retained by Phunthsog Namgyal. The relations between the uncle, Tashi Namgyal and the nephew, Phunthsog Namgyal was very much strained and at one stage an armed clash became imminent. The Cabinet referred the matter to Lhasa, who deputed Lama Kathog Rigzin of Bhutan for mediation between Tashi and Phunthog in 1751 A.D. A great Council was convened at Anle, lasting more than ten months. The members were from all sections of society:

(1) From royal family—9 members.
(2) Dukes or Chos of Purig—8 members.
(3) Cabinet ministers and Lonpo—50 members.
(4) Elders or the Sarpanch—4 members.
(5) Head of Gonpas-Lama—10 members.
(6) Representative of Lhasa Govt.—1 member.
(7) Kashmiri wool and pashmina traders as observers and witnesses—6 members.
Total 88 members.
Chairman Lama Kathog Rigzin.

After deliberations lasting ten months, the Council took the following decisions:

(1) Kharbu dukedom and Spiti valley not to be given to Tashi in addition to Purig area as decided before.

(2) Mulbe and five Chos (dukes) to present their Annual Losar tributes to the Leh king, as customary law.

(3) No intimidation of travellers and traders between Leh and Kashmir, Baltistan, etc.

(4) Ponies taken by force to be returned to the owners in Leh.

(5) No harassment of Kashmiri traders, trade delegations from Delhi and their messengers.

This document, known as "Wam-Le-Ee Chhin-Yig", was executed (and sealed by eighty-eight members) on the 28th day of the fifth month of the Water-Mouse year in the 18th Rale-jung, which works out to the first week of July, 1752 A.D.

Tashi Namgyal of Mulbe died issueless, so Purig Spiti was restored to the Leh kingdom.

Phunthsog Namgyal having retired, Tshewang Namgyal was crowned as king on the 19th day of the third month in the Water Monkey (Ape) year or end of April, 1752 A.D.

TSHEWANG NAMGYAL II, ABOUT 1760-1780

As recorded above, the exact date of crowning of Thsewang is recorded in the Wamle Agreement. As such, Francke's date needs correction. Besides, he has devoted hardly more than two or three paragraphs to Tshewang's reign. Tshewang's misdeeds and lapses may be mentioned here:

(1) He did not abide by the Agreement.

(2) He appointed one Wangyal, stokpa Kalon, a greedy, unscrupulous and perverted offshoot of Gya-Pa-Cho, as his Prime Minister.

(3) Under the influence of one Mirza Malik, a horse dealer, while superficially he behaved as Buddhist, actually he was influenced by Islam. Each year Mirza presented a Badakhshani horse to Tshewang, who had a stud of 500 Badakhshani horses.

(4) He took a low-caste "Bemo"—a dancer of Tshangru Suru—as his wife; the Cabinet Ministers and aristocracy and the people were insulted by "Bemo Bi-bi" and her father Be-kar Nasib Ali Rahim in Leh palace. After a few years, king Tshewang was arrested by the public, deposed and kept under house arrest in Khrigse and Hemis Gonpas. Bemo Bi-bi was nailed down on a door leaf and was exhibited to the public in the main market place of Leh.

The Assembly of people, elders and the ministers decided that

(1) Tshewang be deposed and kept under strict house arrest under stringent conditions.

(2) King Tshewang having listened to and acted on the advice of evil-minded, avaricious and greedy minister Stogpa Kalon Wangyal, disregarding the genuine advice and counsel of faithful Council of Ministers, the queen and the crown prince, he be kept under house arrest in Hemis Gonpa. None of the members of the royal family, ministers and public were to see him in exile or while under house-arrest. He would be entitled to the State usually allotted a prince who takes to clerical habit. He would retain the lucern farm which he purchased from his private funds, for his stud of Badakhshani horses. On his death the entire estate and all property should lapse to Leh palace.

(3) Hemis Gonpas clerical staff and officers were to be responsible for the observance of restrictions and safe custody.

(4) Tshewang should not maintain any old servants.

(5) No extra provision should be sanctioned except the allotted estate.

(6) Tshewang was not to interfere in his son's administration or other affairs of the kingdom.

(7) He should not communicate with the prince Tshetan by letter or verbal message; violation of this condition would invite severe punishment.

(8) He should not resort to malicious black magic or sorcery against his former opponents.

(9) The crown prince, Tshetan, after assuming power, should not take revenge upon the people but should rule with parental love and affection.

(10) The crown prince should expunge or delete all the freshly imposed taxes etc.

(11) Henceforth the ministers, district, town and village officers should not collect extra tax over the traditional tax or levy.

(12) The private or the palace servants should not interfere in the administration of the State, they were to refrain from advising royalty, or council of ministers in appointing State Officers like Ka-lon out of the Lon-pos. (It may be pointed out here that office of a Ka-lon is not hereditary, it is an office. Lon-po is hereditary).

(13) To maintain a high standard of moral environment

in the palace, the household officers, and servants should be selected from the gentry. The wet nurse, male nurse, and the steward of the palace should not accept or transmit any present or applications addressed to the king.

(14) The palace butler, cook, Deo-ri-officer etc., should be appointed by the council of ministers. These servants were to be under direct control of the Minister-in-waiting. The palace servants were to be responsible for discipline, cleanliness, etc., and no stranger or petitioner was to be admitted into the palace without the permission of the officer-in-charge. These drastic measures had to be adopted to stop malpractices, corruption, immorality perpetrated by corrupt palace officials who admitted low-caste Beda, and Bemo dancing girls and *mlechh* into the palace.

(15) People, e.g., aristocracy and proletariat, who go to Hemis gonpa to visit rGyal-Sras-Skyab-gon (one of the princes who joined the ecclesiatical order) should not go to see the deposed ex-king Tshewang. If anybody dared to break those rules, he could be executed on the scaffold and his property would be confiscated.

Signed by Chhag-zod (Steward or Manager) of Hemis Gonpa, all the ministers, aristocracy, elders of Ladakh, Purig, Nubra, Chhor-bat, and witnessed by Kashmir traders.

CHAPTER XI : THE LAST TWO KINGS

This title in Francke's book is incorrect as there were three kings—Tshetan, Tshespal and Tshewang Rab-rTan or Chhog-Sprul, 1782 to 1834.

Tshetan Namgyal : According to the latest research, Tshetan Namgyal ruled for 16 years, from 1782 to 1808 A.D., and not 1780 to 1790, as recorded by Francke. As evident from the Anle Council report, Tshetan was crowned and enthroned at the tender age of ten years, on the 5th day of the 5th month of water-tiger year of 13th Rab-jun or June/July 1782 A.D., and he passed away in 1882 A.D.

Francke makes no mention of invasion of Zanskar by Kulu; most probably he has mixed up the two and thinks that the invasion had taken place in Tshespal's time. In the dedication for the reconstruction of the main gonpas, the name of Tshetan is recorded and not of Tshespal, proving thereby that the invasion took place in Tshetan's time.

Tshespal Namgyal, 1790-1841 : There is a wide difference between Francke and Gergan's estimates in the year and period for which Tshespal ruled. Gergan's dates, 1808 to 1830 A.D., are closer to historical accuracy as these dates are based on uptodate research work, which Francke was not able to procure. Based on the decision taken by Anle Council, Tshespal had to live in the Hemis monastery as a Lama (priest). He did not put on the red habit of the priest but had white under-garments tailored in Lama style. On the death of his brother, he readily ascended the throne and took Palzas Wangmo as his queen. Tshespal had inherited the genes of madness from his father, Tshewang, which he transmitted to his son Chhog-Sprul also. He was well educated, and had a good knowledge of Buddhism but his behaviour and actions were strange and often despicable. He dismissed the old palace servants and appointed new ones, and did not abide by the Anle Agreement. His son, Tshewang Rab-rTan, the crown prince, was more attached to his mother, and had no respect for his father. Knowing this, Tshespal built a new smaller palace for himself to retire when Tshewang Rab-rTan assumed power. Francke is not correct in stating that "The other palace built by Tshespal is the palace of the crown prince of Leh." Francke writes of "the figure of Saint Guru Padma-Od-bar, made of 13 maunds of silver; a white Tara...of nine maunds of silver." He has obviously erred in understanding the measure of weight 'maund' of India=82 lb and Kashmiri measure of 'man' or 'manut'= 30 *tolas* or three-fourths of a pound. Due to proximity of Kashmir and trade relations between Kashmir and Ladakh, the Ladakhi gold, silver or coppersmith, with their Kashmiri background and tradition, used their customary weight, the 'man' equivalent to 30 *tolas* and not the Indian 'man' which was equal to 3,200 *tolas* or 40 'seers.' As such, the weight of silver used for the statues or the stupas are very much exaggerated. This calls for correction.

Francke has mentioned the visit of Moorcraft and Trebeck, but has not referred to the entry of the ruler of Enjan, Abdul Sattar, with 1,600 horsemen into Ladakh to seek shelter and protection from the King of Ladakh. Tshespal betrayed his trust and handed over Abdul Sattar to the Chinese. Sattar, alone and condemned, cursed the king and the people. Perhaps it is a mere coincidence that the curse came true as Ladakh lost its independence and Tshespal died of smallpox in Skardo !

Francke states "As he was the last independent king..." This, again, is incorrect as the independent king was his son Tshewang Rab-rTan alias Chhog Sprul. As already said above Chhog Sprul and Tshespal were not on good terms, so on the advice of the Council of Ministers and the queen, Chhog Sprul was crowned in 1880 A.D. as king, and Tshespal retired and lived at Tingmosgung and Khar-Soma (New Palace) in Leh. On the death of Ka-lon Tshewang Tondub, the administration of the kingdom lapsed into chaos. The Queen Mother, Spalzes Wangmo, and Chhog Sprul interfered in the administration of the Council of Ministers. Rivalry rose among the Chos (dukes or chiefs) of Gya, Mulbe, Paskyum and Trambis. They were divided into two major groups who interfered in the administration and pestered the traders and the goodwill missions passing through their territory. The Queen Mother took the side of Paskyum Cho, her father, and Mulbe Cho. Gyapa Cho sided Trambis Cho, as his brother Namgyal was working as steward or manager of Trambis Cho.

Since ancient times, the Kashmir trade delegation used to travel by the traditional highway—Dras-Skimsha-Kharbu Chhanigund to Kargil—but that year the delegation comprising a Malik and twenty men from Dras, crossed over the Stagpa-la pass into the Suru valley in the jurisdiction of Trambis Cho. The latter objected to the unauthorised passage and a clash ensued, resulting in casualties on both sides. The Malik went to Paskyum Cho, who referred the matter to Leh. On summons from Leh, Trambis Cho and Namgyal Chhogzot pleaded their cause but due to the interference of Spalzes Wangmo, no action was taken against Paskyum Cho, Mulbe Cho and Malik. Trambis Cho, however, felt humiliated. On return from Leh, in order to wreak vengeance on the queen and her aides, he went down to Kishtawar to relate his story to Mohammed Tegh Singh who was related to him by marriage. News of the chaotic conditions in the Ladakh kingdom, the amassed wealth, and the opportune time to annex Ladakh was conveyed to Zorawar Singh, the then general of Raja Gulab Singh of Jammu. Wazir Zorawar Singh, after approval from his master, quietly sneaked through Wardwan valley into the Suru valley without any resistance. The first resistance which Zorawar Singh's army had to encounter was at Karpo Khar. Tashi Wangchug of Sabu village, the Khar-pon (Commander of the fort) and his son fought to the last man before the Dogras captured the fort. Tashi Wangchug of Sabu, his son, and their trusted men were the first contingent to sacrifice their lives in defence of their fatherland.

Chapter XII : The Fall of the Western Tibetan Empire

For invasion of Ladakh by the Dogra Raja of Jammu, Francke has drawn from the stories given by the Dogra officer, Basti Ram. As such, the story is one-sided and biased.

In 1834, Raja Gulab Singh of Jammu thought of extending his dominion towards the north and for this purpose made confidential enquiries from the British and was assured of non-interference. He ordered Wazir Zorawar to march against Ladakh. He was accompanied by his Chief Officers, Sardar Samad Khan, Rana Zalim Singh, Miyan Tota, Wazir Kwaja Bhanjal, Sardar Uttam Singh, Mirza Rasool Beg, Nardap Singh, Imam Malik, Miyan Rai Singh, Basti Ram, Abdul Razakh Singh Mankotia and Syed Madin Shah. His army consisted of 10,000 trained and disciplined soldiers equipped with uptodate weapons. Zorawar marched through Kistwar and reached Purig, a province of Ladakh with headquarters at Kartse. The Ladakh Governor informed the King about the appearance of the enemy. The King deputed Dorje Nyamgal with an army of about 5,000 soldiers.

The Governor of Kartse collected 200 soldiers and for two days kept the Dogras at bay but was finally defeated and killed. The battle was fought on the 16th August 1834. Zorawar prevented his soldiers from destroying crops and harming villagers. His polite conduct was rewarded by submission. He proceeded further and was welcomed by the villagers, who had been assured of safety. A tax of Rs 4 on each house was imposed by him. Though he was opposed by Ladakhi army posts, he removed all resistance and continued to advance unchecked. Sod fell and then Pashkum. Many prisoners were taken and handed over to the garrisons in the forts. In the meanwhile, Dorje Nyamgal arrived with a sizable army of 9,000 men. As snow had fallen, Zorawar wanted to gain time and as such he deputed emissaries to negotiate peace on the condition that a tribute of Rs 10,000 be paid by the King of Ladakh.

The ex-king was ready to accept it when his Queen Zizi insisted on their defending the motherland. A call to arms was given to all Ladakhis. Akabat Mohmud Khan Tshespal, the ex-king of Ladakh, Dorje Namgyal, Rahim Khan of Chhushot and Banka Kahlon joined hands in order to face the invaders. 9,000 Ladakhi soldiers refused to accept Zorawar's terms and started for the defence of Ladakh. Zorawer returned to Lankartse and set about equipping his army with new weapons. As he had nothing for subsistence, he lived on plunder for four months. The Ladakhi army approached but the Wazir knew everything about their movements through his spies. The Ladakhi soldiers, exhausted by their long march, halted for rest. Then suddenly Zorawar led an attack. Bewildered and frantic, the Ladakhis were massacred mercilessly. Many fled towards Leh. 400 were drowned in the river while 1,200 were made prisoners. The Dogras' casualties were 23 killed and 60 wounded.

Ex-king Tshespal lost heart and came to Bazgo along with costly presents and treasures to beg pardon. Both he and Zorawer went to Leh in April 1835 and an agreement was reached by which "Tshespal was installed as a Ruler holding power from Maharaja Gulab Singh," and he promised to pay, besides war indemnity of Rs 50,000, an annual tribute of Rs 20,000. The King paid Rs 37,000 at once, partly in cash and partly in jewellery. Zorawar remained at Leh for four months when news about the recapture of the Fort of Sod by the Ladakhis reached him. By forced marches he reached Suru and defeated the insurgents. 213 Ladakhis were captured and hanged at once. News reached the Wazir that an insurrection had broken at Leh at the instigation of the Sikh Governor of Kashmir, who had despatched a contingent of soldiers.

Tshespal had again been advised by his councillors to attack, but Zorawar's agents informed the Wazir about the conspiracy. By forced marches, Zorawar again appeared and the King expressed his sorrow and regret. He demanded indemnity and took away the property of the royal ladies such as ornaments, gold and silver, utensils, jewellery and other goods. The King was deposed and Nurub Stanzin, a traitor, was designated Governor of Ladakh. The village Stog whose annual revenues amounted to over Rs 1,15,000 was given to him as *jagir*. King Chhog Sprul fled away towards Simla *via* Spiti. All his treasures were confiscated. Zorawar fortified Leh and placed a garrison there under the charge of Miyan Magna, Thanedar. A new fort was built at Leh which was equipped with a garrison of 300 Dogra soldiers under Dalal Singh.

Maharaja Gulab Singh felt displeased with the elevation to Governorship of Nurub Stanzin who had no claim to it. Moreover, the Maharaja wanted to bring Ladakh under his direct control. Zorawar agreed to depose the new Governor on his return to Leh. Tshespal was again installed as a feudatory on the term that he would pay Rs 23,000 as tribute. In the meanwhile, troubles arose in Baltistan on the question of succession to the throne. The Ladakhis, led by Yismalmir and Sukamir, rose again against Dogra rule. Zorawar tried his best to rouse the national spirit against the Dogras but could not gather much support from the people, who were contented because their King Tshespal had been reinstated. Zorawer again marched to Leh and captured Sukamir, who was abused and beaten, his right hand was cut off and the stump was dipped into boiling butter. The hand was fixed on the top of a pole at Khalatse Bridge. Some of the agitators stealthily removed the hand, but for fear of punishment replaced it with that of another corpse. After a few days Sukamir was dragged out of prison and his tongue was cut off. Later he was publicly hanged.

Prince Mohammed Shah of Skardo who had been disinherited by Ahmed Shah Raja of Skardo in favour of his younger brother Mohammed Ali, fled away and approached Zorawar for help and protection. Zorawar was anxious for such an opportunity to use Mohammed Shah as a tool for furtherance of his aims. In 1840 he organised an army of 15,000 men to enslave Baltistan. Ahmed Shah, the Chief of Skardo, remained hidden in his castle, but after twelve days submitted himself to Zorawar.

In the meantime, another freedom fighter, Rahim Khan, the Chief of Chhushot, had raised the banner of rebellion against the intruders. He had issued a call to arms to all Ladakhis against the Dogras. Through the help of Ahmed Shah, Zorawar succeeded in capturing Rahim Khan. He ordered all civilians as well as soldiers to assemble in the big playground of Skardo. Rahim Khan, with some of his fellow-rebels, was escorted by seven soldiers and brought to the middle of the vast ground. "He was admonished to eat much opium, which made him intoxicated. One man brought an armful of wood, another a small pot filled with four pounds of oil. Then three bricks were set up, the small pot was placed on them; a fire was lit and the oil boiled. A man, executioner, appeared and seized Rahim Khan. At first he cut off his hands and dipped the stumps in the hot oil. Then he cut off his tongue and then his ears and showed him to the whole army." Rahim Khan was then pushed into the crowd for display, who beat him and spat at his face. He died in agony after two days. The Balti army was defeated and Mohammed Shah was placed on the throne of Skardo as a tributory of Maharaja Gulab Singh on the promised payment of an annual tribute of Rs 7,000. The Chief of Khaplu and Kartaksha also submitted. Zorawar placed a garrison at Skardo. Ahmed Shah, along with his favourite son and several other Chieftains were carried off as prisoners of war. All treasures were carried away.

Tshespal Namgyal, who accompanied Zorawar Singh as a royal prisoner, died of small-pox in Skardo. He had suffered bitter indignity. His body was brought to Stog and cremated. Henceforth, Ladakh became a part of Dogra territory. Francke has not recorded the story of vandalism perpetrated by Zorawar Singh, his army officers and the rank and file, who despoiled and looted all the valuable property, religious utensils, statues of the Buddha and other deities, stupas (chhod-tran) from palaces, forts and gonpas and temples, right from the Kailash to Baltistan excepting two, the temple at Kocharnath and Hemis Gonpa. Hemis Gonpa was saved because the wise Chhagzot (Steward or Manager) promised to bear all the expenses and be the Commissariat for the Dogra army. In their avarice, they even removed one arm of the Buddha (in gilt copper) from Shay Khar-Chung (palace). It was restored by Jigmed, Chhog Sprul's son. The Dogra soldiers did not stop at the looting of silver, gold, copper, silk, and precious stones; they also pulled down the famous University Hall and printing press at Leh, Gonpas, Khar-Soma built by Tshespal and the mansions of Ka-lon and Lonpos, and used the material in the construction of Leh fort at Skara, barracks, quarters for their civil administrative staff. In place of birch-bark for mud-roofing, they used leaves of religious texts written on parchment paper, ordinary paper and the Tantric mantras printed on birch bark. The traces of vandalism perpetrated by the Dogras are still visible after a lapse of more than a century.

Invasion of Tibet and Revolt in Ladakh

Zorawar had now subdued the whole of Ladakh and Baltistan and considered himself invincible. He was elated with success and thought of invading Central Asian States but later on abandoned this idea in favour of Tibet. He had two reasons for this project. "The plunder of the Tibetan monasteries which were known to possess gold and jewels would enrich his soldiers and secondly conquest of Tibet would highly please Gulab Singh." Zorawar Singh, on his return from Baltistan in the spring of 1840, busied himself in planning, mobilising and organising an army of about 6,000 to invade Tibet. Chhagzot Gonbo was appointed as the Commissariat General for collection of 3,000 maunds of wheat flour and *tsampa* and its regular despatch to the front. Zorawar's army of 6,000 was a conglomeration of 3,000 Dogras, the rest Balti, Purigpa and Ladakh. Zorawar divided this army into two columns, one under Mian Rai Singh, and the other under his own command. A smaller contingent was sent under Ghulam Khan of Chhushod to Spiti where his uncle was Dogra governor of Spiti and Lahul. He had instructions to capture Chhumurti, Guge and Tshaprang at the time signal.

In the last week of May 1841, Zorawar and his column

crossed the Changla and proceeded to Rudok. The frontier guard of Rudok castle and the civilians along with their animals had entrenched themselves in the fort. Crossfiring continued for some days. Mehta Ram, with two suicide squads, under the cover of fire and natural protection, made a bid to scale the fortification. Tibetan guards realising their own small strength, limited food, fodder, water and the overwhelming force of the Dogra invaders sent a messenger for negotiation for ceasefire and truce. Zorawar readily accepted the proposal. The next day the inmate of the castle, lay and lama officials, came out with presents to Zorawar Singh which pleased him immensely. Rudok rZong was taken over and handed to Lonpo Chhogdar of Tangtse, who was appointed by Zorawar Singh as the Commander of the fort, alongwith a force of 30 Dogra soldiers and 50 others. Zorawar proceeded to Gartok (Gar) as scheduled to meet Rai Singh's column. Mian Rai Singh's column proceeded to Demchog via Rupsho Anle, encountered no opposition at the border—Demchog—and advanced by easy marches and camped three miles short of Tashigang gonpa. For two days all was quiet; on the third day the scouts informed that the Tibetans were preparing for a night attack. At dusk, the guards of the O.P. detected some movements at a distance. Sniper Sonam, Bazgo Kalon scared the Tibetans by shooting two of their men. The Tibetans, lay and lama, closeted themselves inside the fortification of the gonpa. The captain of the frontier guard, who was strolling along the parapet wall of the gonpa, was shot dead by Sonam. This incident combined with the overwhelming might of the Dogra army, made the Tibetan frontier guards realise that they would not be able to hold for long with their ancient muskets and limited provisions and water. Thus, they sent a couple of men to negotiate for truce. Rai Singh accepted the conditions and captured the gonpa without arresting or harming the besieged people. He proceeded to Gartok to join his leader Zorawar Singh. The Tashigang frontier guards were detailed to construct a fort of Dogra design and plan.

The combined force of Zorawar Singh and Rai Singh halted at Gartok for 13 days. The inhabitants of the area, including those of Menser village, had fled; not a soul could be found in this vast wilderness. They proceeded towards the Kailash. At Tok-po-ral-sum (confluence of three streams or valleys), the local Changpa, Dogpa and Chagpa (who live by hunting, extortion or plundering), numbering about 800 strong, had mustered to ambush the invaders. Zorawar's scouts failed to detect the Tibetans. During the night, the Tibetans attacked the Dogra camp. In the ensuing fight which lasted till dawn, heavy casualties were sustained by both sides. Zorawar proceeded to Kailash where he recorded the history of the Kailash and Manasarovar as dictated by the in-charge Lama. He took a vow to install a Devi made of copper and gold. At Kailash, Zorawar's wife (Boo-wa-jee or elder sister) arrived from Leh under the escort of 20 Dogra soldiers, 10 Ladakhis and Onpo Rigzin and Tshetan Dorje. They also brought 300 maunds of wheat flour. Henceforth, Onpo Rigzin was made responsible for Boo-wa-jee's comfort and safe escort to Kashmir. Zorawar's wife circumambulated both Kailash and Manasarovar. She had the ritual bath in the lake and made a votive offering of precious stones, pearls, gold and silver to the lake. After a rest of two days she was sent back to Kashmir, chaperoned by Onpo Rigzin and 30 armed men.

Zorawar and his army proceeded to Purang after posting soldiers at strategic points such as Menser and Kardam. *En route* there was no resistance as the people, generally nomads of various classes, had fled to the Purang area with all their belongings. It was only in Kardam village that they found some grains left behind as they had not completed harvesting and threshing of corn. The villagers were in a panic, the leaders had fled. Zorawar ordered that nobody should be harmed or persecuted. In a defile at Tog-sar, Zorawar's army was waylaid by about 100 Tibetans who enfiladed them with rifle fire. There were some casualties. The Dogra army counter-attacked the Tibetans with guns and swords till they fled. On reaching Taklakot, they dug trenches and built pallisades to guard their camp and water supply. On the fifth day of their arrival, 100 picked 'sipahis' entered the lama residence situated below the main fort. Some people were shot dead or wounded by the Tibetan fire. During the night another 300 soldiers joined them. After some days of seige, shortage of water in the fort became acute. The Tibetan leaders came out of the fort with presents to Zorawar Singh in token of submission and surrender. On September 6, 1841, the Dogras took over Taklakot fort and Mehta Basti Ram and a 100 soldiers were stationed in the fort to guard this strategic point. The Dogras built another fort in the valley, in the vicinity of a water supply, to stock provisions received from Leh, Spiti and the local inhabitants. Zorawar himself proceeded to see the famous temple of Kochar Nath, where he offered his own gold *kantha* or locket.

In the meanwhile, at a pre-arranged signal, Ghulam and his uncle at Spiti invaded Chhumurti, Guge province, and captured Tshaprang, Tholing and Tarba forts, and brought valuable loot of the gonpas to please their Dogra masters. The people of Taklakot were asked to pay a sum of Rs 10,000 in Indian currency only. Ten leaders were detained in the Dogra camp as hostages till the amount was paid. The Tibetans were able to collect only Rs 1,800 in Indian currency, another Rs 1,400 was obtained by selling the religious utensils of the gonpa to Bhotias of Kumaon; for the rest of the amount they took away from the people and the gonpa all the valuables—China silk dresses, utensils, muskets, carpets, 120 maunds of China tea (60 pony loads). Out of the gold, copper and brass collected, a statue of "Ganesh" was made in gilt copper in high relief, by Palle goldsmiths.

The Dogra conquest of Naris-skor-sum alarmed the Nepalese. The Kathmandu Darbar sent a fact-finding delegation to the border. Zorawar Singh gave a warm reception to the delegation who stayed for about a week and departed after an exchange of gifts. When the Dogras took the administration into their own hands, they asked the inhabitants to sell wool, pashmina and shahtoosh only to the Ladakhi traders and not to the Bhotias of Garhwal and Kumaon. The frontier guards and other agencies of the British informed them about the administration and arrival of the delegation from Nepal. The British government was considerably perturbed by the collusion of Nepal and Zorawar Singh in their attempt to form an anti-British alliance. The stoppage of wool trade with the Bhotias of United province of Indian government was another source of apprehension.

Zorawar proceeded further and encamped at Tirthapori on the Sutlej river. A Tibetan force numbering 10,000 soldiers arrived on the spot. News about the arrival of a further army came from Mehta Basti Ram, who had been posted at *Takla Khar* on the river *Gogra* near the Nepal frontier. One night there was very heavy snowfall and many soldiers died. A severe winter had set in and Zorawar realised the danger of utter annihilation. He deputed a small force of 600 men under Ghulam Khan to face the Tibetans, but it was surrounded by the Tibetan army and cut to pieces. He had no alternative but to attack. On December 10, 1841, he led an attack on the Tibetan army. The fighting continued for three days. He said, "Either the Tibetans will take my head or I shall take it myself!" Wounded by a bullet in the thigh, he fell to the ground with his sword in his hand and fought fiercely to the end. A javelin pierced his heart and he died. His dead body was cut into pieces by the Tibetans who carried off his head and pieces of his flesh as souvenirs. It is said that they pulled out his hair and kept it for the sake of good fortune. Thus died the fearless man. Having lost their leader, his soldiers fled away in order to save their lives but most of them were killed. Only about a 1,000 escaped alive. The Tibetans pursued the fleeing Dogra soldiers and 700 were captured and despatched to Tibet. Among the prisoners were Ahmed Shah of Baltistan, General Rai Singh, Ghulam Khan and Nono Sodnam and Prince Ali Mohammed.

After Zorawar's death, the Tibetans sent a warning to Ladakh to prepare for war. It produced adverse political reaction in Ladakh. The Government of India became anxious and Captain Cunningham, Assistant to the British Resident, was asked to proceed to Ladakh to negotiate for an amicable settlement. Mehta Magana sent a plea for help to Gulab Singh who despatched a new and better equipped army of 8,000 soldiers under Dewan Hari Chand and Wazir Ratnu. A call to arms was issued to Ladakh and Baltistan. The peasants were ordered to mobilise for transport work. The attack was launched and fort after fort was taken by the Dogra army. The Tibetan army was pursued. They were either killed or captured at different forts. But the Tibetan government sent 3,000 soldiers to invade

Ladakh. Both the armies met at Drangste. On the advice of Thanpa sodnam, the stream was dammed up by the Dogra army with the result that the Tibetan camp was flooded. Their arms and ammunition became wet. After a fierce battle the Tibetans suffered defeat. Their Commander Ragasha was captured and his head was severed with a sword. Besides Peshi and Zurkhan fifty others were taken prisoner. Peshi committed suicide by swallowing his diamond ring. The Tibetans agreed to make peace.

By now, the British government had become alarmed and directed Gulab Singh to cease all hostilities. They deputed Cunningham to Ladakh. The old boundary between Ladakh and Tibet was re-established and it was agreed to provide facilities for trade. Exchange of prisoners was also agreed to. "Then those Sinpas (Dogras) who had been kept captive in Tibet had married Tibetan women. They all went to Khacul (Kashmir), everyone carrying a child. Those Tibetans who had been taken captive by the Sinpas (Dogras) had married women of Hijambhu (Jammu). They went back to Tibet, carrying two or three children each." Some of the prisoners who had now settled at Lhasa refused to leave Tibet.

"*Dewan Hari Chand* promised to reinstate all the Tibetan Ministers and the Ladakhi King and Queen with their whole court." But this promise was not kept and the whole of Ladakh was annexed. The Dewan abolished the whole nobility and Rigzin Onpo was made responsible to the Maharaja. The Leh garrison was doubled and Miyan Magna was left at Leh.

The above account has been constructed from the Tibetan as well as Ladakhi sources, not available to Francke. The private diaries of the Secretaries of the last three kings of Ladakh, Tshespal, Chhog Sprul, and Jigmed Namgyal and the records of the hermit Lama have been reproduced now.[18]

18. For further details see S.S. Gergan, *Ladags-rGyalrabs Chimed Ster.*

A History of Western Tibet

A.H. Francke

A History of Western Tibet

Introduction

THE reader of the history of Western Tibet will probably like to know from what sources the information regarding this topic has been drawn. The sources are of two kinds: some are foreign, and some Western Tibetan. The latter are of the greatest interest to us, and are of a two-fold character: we possess records on stone as well as on paper. Of the former, which cover the time from 200 B.C.-1900 A.D., only comparatively little has become known up to the present, the reason being that systematic and thorough researches in that domain have not yet been made. Also, regarding the records on paper, although what is probably the most important work, the chronicles of the kings of Leh (or Ladakh), has been edited, much remains to be done. I have heard of the existence of the following historical works which have never yet been examined by a European: the chronicles of the vassal-chiefs of Chigtan;[1] the chronicles of the village of Sakti; and the "history of the monasteries," as it is found, I am told, in the *Bidur* (Vaidurya) *gserpo*. It is very probable that there are many more historical works in existence in the country, the names of which will be discovered in course of time. Besides these books, some villages are in possession of shorter documents on paper, in particular edicts of several kings, to collect and edit which will be a necessary preliminary to a scientific study of our history. One of these documents, an edict by King Nyima namgyal, will be found translated in these pages.

1. The present ex-chief of Chigtan tells me, however, that the only existing MS. of this historical work was lost during his lifetime.

Let us now examine the general character of Ladakh historiography, especially the chronicles of Ladakh on which the following history is chiefly based. The chronicles, so far as they are made use of here, cover the time from 900—1842 A.D. But as the historiography did not stop with the loss of independence of the kingdom, but has been continued down to the present, the Ladakhi chronicles comprise a full millennium by this time. The character of the work is not the same during the different periods it describes. Its most ancient part can hardly be called a history; nor was it apparently meant to be such. It was begun as a pedigree of the kings of Leh, whose chief intention it was to prove their descent from the famous line of the ancient kings of Lhasa. Thus the first portion of the work, covering roughly the period of 900—1400 A.D., does not contain much besides mere names. About the year 1400 the account begins to become fuller. This may be due to the fact that the second dynasty branched off at about that time, and this new line of kings may have had a stronger instinct for history. At any rate, the accounts grow in fulness after 1400 A.D. Still, they leave much to be desired from a European point of view. The writers were Lamas, and to them the greatest events during the reign of a king were his presents to Lamas and monasteries, or his building of chortens and mani walls. Much ink has been expended on these events, which are of very little interest to the average European. On the other hand, the campaigns of the kings are treated with extraordinary brevity, and of their economical work we hear nothing at all. Only in the case of the last few kings are we able to form an idea of their characters, and of tactics employed during the campaigns we hear nothing. The historian is quite satisfied with telling us the final result of the campaign. Thus we see that all those points which go to make a history of a country serviceable are missing in these Western Tibetan records; and yet, the naive tone of the historians has often a charm of its own.

An important question is this: Do the Ladakhi historians tell the truth, or is their history entirely or partially fabricated matter ? The best test of the veracity of an historical account is its comparison with other entirely independent documents. Only in a very few cases are we able to compare a Western

Missing Page

statements, even with regard to chronology, and I think we have a right to accept also the first part of the history as on the whole true and reliable.

In no case do the Western Tibetan chronicles enable us to fix the time of the reign of a king exactly. As, however, several kings were contemporaries of other historical personalities, whose dates can be fixed, we are in a position to furnish all the Ladakhi kings with approximate dates. With regard to the second dynasty, eventual mistakes can hardly amount to more than a decade. From the outset it must be understood that the reign of a certain king may have been longer or shorter than the period given in this history; but it is probable that some years of his actual reign coincide with some of the years given here. The fixed dates on which hinges the whole chronology given in this book are the following: Langdarma, 900—921 A.D.; Tsongkapa, the contemporary of King Bum Lde, 1378-1441 (or 1355-1418) A.D.; the Balti war, under Jamyang namgyal, 1580-1600 A.D., according to Cunningham, probably from Mohammedan sources; the siege of Basgo, 1646-47 A.D., under Delegs namgyal; and the Dogra wars, 1834-1842 A.D. The longest period without a fixed date is 900 to about 1400 A.D. It is filled up by assigning to each of the kings twenty-five years. According to European conceptions, the average duration of a generation is thirty years. But as the Tibetans marry rather early, the duration of a generation may be shorter here.

The most important foreign documents which are of particular value for a history of Western Tibet are: (1) The Rajatarangini (chronicles of Kashmir) by Kalhana, for the Chinese and Kashmiri expeditions to Western Tibet, in the beginning of the eighth century; (2) the annals of the Chinese Tang dynasty, for the same period; (3) the Rajatarangini (chronicles of Kashmir) by Jonaraja, for the career of Rinchana Bhoti, in the beginning of the fourteenth century; (4) the account of the Mogul historian, Mir Izzet Ullah, for details about the siege of Basgo, 1646-1647; (5) the account of the Dogra war, 1834-1839, by Basti Ram, a Dogra officer, communicated by Cunningham; (6) Central Tibetan historical works in several instances.

In the following, the literature which has been made use of

for the individual chapters is enumerated :

Chapter I. *Ladak*, by General Sir Alexander Cunningham. *Memoir on the Ancient Geography of Kashmir*, by M.A. Stein, Ph.D., etc.

Chapter II. *Kleine archaologische Ertrage einer Missionsreise nach Zangskar*, von A.H. Francke, Z.D.M.G., 1906.

Chapter III. "The Eighteen Songs of the Bonona Festival", by A.H. Francke, *Indian Antiquary*, 1905. *Notes on a Language Map of Western Tibet*, by A.H. Francke, J.A.S.B., 1904.

Chapter IV. *Memoir on the Ancient Geography of Kashmir*, by M.A. Stein, Ph.D., etc. (Chavannes' edition of the Tang annals was not at my disposal.)

Chapter V. "Archaeological Notes on Balumkhar", by A.H. Francke, *Indian Antiquary*, 1905. *Der Fruhlings und Wintermythus der Kesarsage*, von A.H. Francke : Helsingfors, 1901-1903. "A Lower Ladakhi Version of the Kesarsaga," by A.H. Francke, *Bibliotheca Indica*, 1905, ff.

Chapter VI. *Three Documents relating to the History of Ladakh*, by K. Marx, J.A.S.B. : 1891. *The Valley of Kashmir*, by Sir Walter Lawrence (for Rinchana Bhoti).

Chapter VII. *Three Documents relating to the History of Ladakh*, by K. Marx, J.A.S.B., 1901. "The Rock-inscriptions at Mulbe", by A.H. Francke, *Indian Antiquary*, 1906.

Chapter VIII. *Three Documents relating to the History of Ladakh*, by K. Marx, J.A.S B. : First and Second Documents, 1891 and 1894. *Ladak*, by Sir Alexander Cunningham.

Chapter IX. *Three Documents relating to the History of Ladakh*, by K. Marx, J.A.S.B. : Second Document, 1894. *Ladak*, by Sir Alexander Cunningham.

Chapter X. *Three Documents relating to the History of Ladakh*, by K. Marx, J.A.S.B : Second Document, 1894. "Some Historical Inscriptions and Documents from Western Tibet", by A.H. Francke, *Indian Antiquary*, 1906 : in course of preparation (for Nyima namgyal).

Chapter XI. *Three Documents relating to the History of Ladakh*, by K. Marx, J.A.S.B. : Second Document, 1894. *Die Geschichte des fruheren Konigs von Ladakh, etc.*, von Theodora Francke, 1903.

Chapter XII. *Three Documents relating to the History of*

Ladakh, by K. Marx, J.A.S.B. : Third Document, 1902. *Ladak*, by Sir Alexander Cunningham.

Chapter XIII. *Ladak*, by Sir Alexander Cunningham. *Die Geschichte des fruheren Konigs von Ladakh, etc.*, von Theodora Francke, 1903.

Chapter XIV. *Three Documents relating to the History of Ladakh*, by K. Marx, J.A.S.B. : Third Document, 1902. *Die Geschichte des frutheren Konigs von Ladakh, etc.*, by Theodora Francke, 1903. *Ladak*, by Sir Alexander Cunningham.

Throughout : *Ladakhi Songs*, edited by A.H. Francke, in co-operation with Rev. S. Ribbach and Dr F.E. Shawe. *Erste Sammlung tibetischer historischer Inschriften auf Felsen und Steinen, von West Tibet*, von A.H. Francke, 1906.

FOR SUCH AS WOULD LIKE TO USE THIS HISTORY AS A GUIDE-BOOK, THE FOLLOWING LIST WILL PROVE USEFUL.

Dras—Ancient Buddhist sculptures. Modern Dogra castle near the Bungalow. Ruins of unknown castles on the low hills in the valley. Rock-carvings.

Shimsha Karbu—Ruined castle of unknown origin. Rock-carvings.

Kargil—Sod castle, north of Kargil. Branch off to Suru River. Ruins of Kartse castle. Modern Dogra castle in the town.

Pashkyum—Ruins of castle.

Mulbe—First Buddhist monastery on the road. On the rock, ancient inscriptions. Colossal sculpture of Maitreya.

Bod Kharbu—Ancient town on the hill above the village, with inscription, Stagtse castle. Branch off to Chigtan River. Chigtan, ancient monastery and castle. Shagkar castle.

Henasku—Castle and kings of, Lamayuru. Ancient monastery. Branch off to Wanla. Ancient castle. Hunupata, Dard rock-carvings.

Kalatse—Ancient inscriptions near bridge. Bragnag castle. Dard castles Balukar.

Nyurla—Branch off to Tingmogang. Famous residence of the Ladakhi kings. Ancient sculptures.

Saspola—Near the bridge. ancient castle of Alchi Kargog. Rock-inscriptions. Cave monastery, Nyizlapug. On left bank of the Indus, Alchi, with ancient monastery.

Basgo—Ancient fortress. Monastery inside castle. Kashmir monastery. Battle of Basgo. Mani-walls. Branch off to Likir, famous monastery.

Nyemo—Ruined nunnery; sculpture of ancient abbess. Chungkar castle.

Daru—Ancient castle. Sculpture with inscription, on the trade road.

Phiang—Famous monastery. Ruins of castles.

Spitug—Famous monastery. Kaoche monastery in ruins.

Leh—Longest mani-wall. Castle of Trashi namgyal in ruins. Palace of Sengge namgyal. Largest chorten in ruins. Red college, on the Namgyal tsemo hill. Mosques. Ruined monastery, on elephant crag. Many ancient Buddhist sculptures on stone.

Sabu—Castles, etc.

Sheh—Castle, chorten. Huge image. Ancient inscriptions.

Chushod—Balti colony.

Hemis—Monastery.

Chemre—Monastery.

Rongchurgyud—Dard colony.

Hanle—Monastery.

Trashisgang, beyond the frontier. Famous monastery.

In Baltistan.

Skardo—Famous castle. *Sadpor*, ancient Buddhist sculptures and inscriptions. *Kapulu*, chief of.

IN ZANGSKAR.

Spadum, castle of. Ancient Buddhist sculptures. *Zangla*, castle and kings of. *Stongrdze*, ancient chortens. *Kanika*, monastery.

I

Greek and Roman Authors on the Nations of Western Tibet

THE present population of Western Tibet is the result of a long process of blending of at least three distinct peoples, two of which are of Aryan stock, whilst one, which is numerically superior to the other two, is of Mongolian origin. The Aryan nations are : the Dards of Gilgit, and the Mons of North India (perhaps from Kashmir). The Mongolian is the Tibetan nation.

After this statement let us turn to Herodotus, and see what he has to say about the Dards; for, although in his description of the different kinds of Indians (*Lib.* iii. 98-106) he does not give the name of the Dards, authorities are practically agreed that what he says about the country of the "gold-digging ants" refers to the land of the present Dards on the Indus. He says in *Lib.* iii. 102 : "Another kind of Indians live in the neighbourhood of the town Kaspatyros, and the land Paktyika (Afghanistan—the Greek word corresponds to the modern words Pashtu and Pathan), away towards the north from the rest of the Indians; their way of living is about the same as that of the Bactrians. These are the most warlike of all the Indians, and it is they who are sent for gold; for in this district there is the sandy desert. In this desert and in this sand there are ants which are smaller than dogs, but larger than foxes; for some which were caught there are now in the possession of the King of Persia. These ants make for themselves burrows below ground, and in doing so throw up the earth, as ants do with us, and in the same manner; they also look exactly like ours. This thrown-up sand contains the gold, and for the sake of this sand the Indians are sent into the desert...104. The Indians, after having harnessed their camels in such a way, ride for the gold, taking the precaution to rifle the gold during the heat of the day, because at that time the ants disappear underneath the ground.. 105. When the Indians arrive at the place (of the gold-dust) with their leather bags, they fill these bags with sand and ride away as quickly as possible. For the ants, which, as the Persians tell, have found out what has happened through their sense of smell, are at once after them, and they are exceedingly swift. Thus, if the Indians do not gain a good start before the ants have gathered, none of them would be able to escape...."

Quite a similar story is told by Megasthenes, the Greek Ambassador at an Indian court, who relates that the Indian ants dug gold out of the earth, not for the sake of metal, but in making burrows for themselves.

I have given Herodotus' story almost in full, because it is of particular interest as an example of the continuity of such tales. For several years I lived at the little village of Kalatse, which is now thoroughly Tibetanised, but was a Dard colony in former days. Here I received a letter from a European student of folklore,[1] asking me to send him tales of gold-digging ants, if such should be current in the place. After a few days I was able to send him two long tales of gold-digging ants, discovered at Kalatse. But not only that : I was even shown the kind of ant which, according to the belief of the Kalatse people, was the gold-digger. It was a very tiny creature, and far from the size of a dog or fox; but we must allow the story to have grown a little on its way from India to Greece.

Putting aside this fable, the fact remains that the existence of the Upper Indus valley as a gold-producing country has been known to the world since the times of Herodotus. Other classical authors speak of the gold-production of this district. Ctesias states that "the gold was not obtained by washing, as in the river Pactolus"; and Pliny's sentence, *Fertilissimi sunt auri Dardae, Setae vero argenti* ("the country of the Dards

1. Dr B. Laufer.

produces much gold, but that of the Setae much silver" : Pliny, *Lib* vi., c. 19), has become quite famous, because his tribe of the Setae seems to be none other than the Indian caste of bankers, who are called *Seth* (Cunningham).

Even in our part of the country it is of particular interest to go along the banks of the Indus and to observe the traces which the gold-diggers have left there from days of old. I have travelled along the Indus from Saspola to Dartsig, a distance of over fifty miles, and have seen but few parts of the ground which have remained untouched. It looks as if the ground had been worked with huge ploughs. In many places remnants of masonry can still be seen in the earth. There has been a break in the digging for several years, owing to political causes; but the eyes of Europeans are once more directed towards these ancient gold-fields, and the old river may yet witness once more the feverish activity of human gold-hunters. The colour of the gold found here is of a bright yellow, so bright that the natives are not at once ready to believe that the gold generally used by Europeans is the genuine metal.

The Kashmiris were known to the Greeks and Romans by name. Ptolemy speaks of the region of *Kaspeiria,* which he places between the *Daradrai* (Dards) on the Indus, and the *Kylindrine* (the present Kulu) on the Byas. The Greek word *Kaspeiria* would represent the Greek attempt at writing the Indian word Kasvira, which, though not occurring in literature, must be supposed to be the middle stage between the Sanskrit word Kasmira and the modern dialectical word Kasir. Another later Greek writer, Dyonysios, mentions the tribe of the *Kaspeiroi,* who in his time were famous among Indians for their feet, *i.e.*, their mountaineering capacities.

All the rivers which irrigate the district of Western Tibet and its surroundings were known to the ancients, especially to Ptolemy. The Sanskrit name of the Jhelum is *Vitasta,* and Ptolemy calls it *Bidaspes* (instead of the more ancient *Hydaspes*). The Indus was known under its present name. The Sutlej, in Sanskrit *Satadru,* is called *Zaradros* by Ptolemy; the Byas River (Sanskrit *Vipasa*), *Bibasis* (instead of the more ancient *Hyphasis*); and the Chandra Bhaga appears as *Sandabal* in Ptolemy's book.

General Cunningham also places the tribe of the *Cesi* (Pliny) and the *Akhassa regio* of Ptolemy in the district of Western Tibet; but as these assumptions have not yet been examined by modern scholars, I must leave these questions undecided.

Ptolemy, who even mentions the nation of the *Byltae* (which sounds very much like Balti), of whom he says that they lived in the west of the *Akhassa regio*, is the geographer of old who is credited with having preserved to us an ancient name of the Tibetans He speaks of the nation of the *Dabasae*, and this has suggested itself to Tibetan scholars as being a Roman transliteration of the modern province of U (spelt dBus) in Central Tibet. There exists a very strange law of pronunciation in the Tibetan language, according to which the letters *d* and *b* annul each other, if they meet at the beginning of a word. Thus, the Tibetan *dBus* would have to be pronounced *us*, and as a final *s* can become an *i*, the last stage in the changing pronunciation of the long word *dBus* is *U*. This law of sound is so strange that many philologists have had difficulty in accepting it. They say that the real word had always been *U* or *Us*, and that the prefixing of the letters *d* and *b* must have been the work of some fantastical scholar. In answer to these doubts other philologists went as far back as Ptolemy, and proved with his ancient *Dabasae* that in his days the *d* and *b* of the word *dBus* must have had their full sound. However this may be, the West Tibetan dialects of the present day, which have a very archaic character, provide ample proof that the *d* and *b* which annul each other nowadays in most Tibetan dialects must have been a reality in ancient times.

It is with the help of these dialects that the fact of the existence of Tibetans in Western Tibet in olden times—say, in the days of Herodotus—is established. Otherwise, we should feel inclined to say that the country was in the hands of the Dards and Mons alone till the advent of the Central Tibetan dynasty in 1000 A.D. But in that case the Tibetan language of Western Tibet would show the characteristics of Central Tibetan, which were fully developed as early as 700 A.D.

Philological reasons compel us to believe that in the times of Herodotus, when the Dards and Mons had probably not yet left their original homes, an ancient tribe of Tibetan nomads tended their herds on the plains and hills of Western Tibet. Cunningham believes them to have extended as far as Gilgit. Their life probably in no way differed from that of Tibetan nomads of the present day. They lived in tents of yak-hair, on the produce of their numerous herds of yaks, goats and sheep, and chased the *Kiang*, the wild sheep, and the wild yak; for in those times all these animals seem to have had their feeding grounds a long way further to the west than they have nowadays, if rock-carvings and folklore do not deceive us. These ancient *Dabasae* had probably the poetical instinct as strongly marked as their present children, and similar songs to the one given here in Major Peacock's version of my translation (*Ladakhi Songs*, No. VII.) may have sounded through the valleys and hills of ancient Ladakh.

A maiden tending flocks on a mountain-side sings across the valley to a youth similarly employed :

In the meadow, in the meadow, in the higher meadow blows—
Oh listen, lad, oh listen to my song—
A flower, far the sweetest that in field and garden grows—
Oh listen, lad, oh listen to my song.
Thou mayst cull the flower, sweetheart, thou mayst cull the tender flower,
But thou shalt not grasp it rudely in thine hand ;
Else 'twill wither in a moment, 'twill be perished in an hour,
If thou, ruthless, dare to seize it in thine hand.
Oh, but, lean thy bosom t'wards it, it will nestle to thy soul,
It will cling with tend'rest tendrils round thine heart ;
Ah, lad, lean thy bosom t'wards it, it will grow into thy soul,
And with strong, yet tender tendrils, hold thine heart.

2

The Mission of the Mons to Western Tibet

In almost every Western Tibetan village we find one or several families who are called *Mon*. Those people are mostly musicians or carpenters, and are treated with little respect by the rest of the population. Their low position makes us believe that they belong to a nation, originally different from the Tibetans, who were conquered in former days. But to find out who the Mons really were is impossible in most parts of Ladakh, because there, after the settlement of the Mons, and before the arrival of the Central Tibetans, the migrations of the Dards took place, and thus the recollections of the people have been obscured. It is different with Zangskar. Zangskar has apparently never been colonised by Dards, and the course of events there is not so complicated. On a journey to Zangskar I discovered the following interesting items with regard to the tribe of the Mons :

Zangskar, I was told by the inhabitants, was once entirely in the hands of the Mons. The ruins of their old castles are still called "Mon-castles." Then the country was conquered by the Tibetans, and remained a Tibetan country until the Mons came back about seventy years ago and reconquered it. I learned that in Zangskar all Indians, Kashmiris, or Dogras, are called Mon; and if the Indians of the present day are called so it becomes very probable that also the ancient Mons, who were subjected by the Tibetans, were an Indian tribe. And who would not think of Kashmiris in the first place, because they are the next neighbours to Zangskar? Among the ruins of the settlements of the ancient Mons of Zangskar I discovered imposing remains of ancient Buddhist art, and more and more the conviction grew upon me that the settlement of the ancient Mons in Zangskar and Ladakh must have had some connection with the pre-Lamaist Buddhism. The strongest proof of the colonisation of Western Tibet by ancient Indians are inscriptions in Brahmi characters of about 200 B.C. We know that at the legendary third Buddhist Council, which, according to tradition, was held by King Asoka (272—231 B.C.) at Pataliputra, it was resolved to send Buddhist missionaries to Yarkand, Kashmir, and many other countries. Buddhism got such a firm hold in Kashmir that the fourth legendary Council, under King Kanishka (125—152 A.D.), is said to have been held at Jalandhara in Kashmir. Either after the third or the fourth Council Buddhism must have been carried to Western Tibet, situated between Kashmir and Yarkand And, as the case of the Mons shows plainly, the mission cannot have been a religious mission only—it was apparently a civilising and colonising mission as well. It would have been difficult to influence the wandering nomads without founding centres of Buddhist teaching with temples and monasteries. The almost empty land attracted more and more colonists, and the religious settlements grew into villages and towns in course of time.

The following is a short description of the ancient Buddhist remains at *Spadum* in Zangskar. On the slope of the ridge towards the river, a little below the town, there is a huge boulder of at least the size of a two-storied Ladakhi house. On the north side, looking towards the town, there is a sculpture of the five figures of Buddhas in deep relief, which are locally known as *rGyalba rigs lnga.* The figures are all much above life-size, and the sculptures, together with all adjuncts, cover a space of at least six yards square. In many cases the relief is worked out of the rock to a depth of fifteeen centimetres, and altogether the workmanship is better than that of any other ancient sculpture in Western Tibet. The figure of the Buddha in the middle represents Maitreya, the future Buddha of the next *Kalpa* (cycle of 100,000 years), and the four other Buddhas are said to be representations of the Buddhas of the present and the three preceding Kalpas Maitreya is the only figure which is furnished with a crown with three points. Like the others, he is seated on a lotus-throne, and underneath his throne there are two lions. His hands almost touch each other in front, but his right hand is a little above the left. The Buddha to the left of Maitreya has a pair of peacocks under his throne, and his finger-tips touch each other in front. The second to the left of Maitreya has two *garudas* (mythological birds) underneath his throne. He holds up his right hand as if in the act of teaching. The two Buddhas on the right of Maitreya both touch the ground with their right hands. What symbols they have under their lotus-thrones cannot be determined, as that part of the sculpture is covered with earth. Underneath the pictures of these five Buddhas there is a long row of pyramidical chaityas, and below them a row of men who all wear hats with three points, like Maitreya. Above the five Buddhas, at both ends of the row, there are two square recesses bored into the rock, which evidently served for the reception of beams. Thus it appears that there used to be a hall erected in front of the boulder, and that the sculptures formed the back wall of the hall. Besides the sculptures described above, there are a host of other pictures—standing Buddhas of six yards high, and chaityas of all sizes, carved on the same rock in other places and in a less deep style of relief.

A little higher up the river, on the slope, there is a similar boulder, on which there are more sculptures, in low relief. They represent five standing Buddhas, probably the same which we found in a sitting posture on the previous rock. And underneath three of them the outlines of figures of lions, peacocks, and *garudas* can be seen. These emblems were probably added at a much later date; otherwise, emblems would have been carved also underneath the two remaining Buddhas. The artist did not know what to add there, because in his time that portion of the principal sculpture was apparently already covered with earth. On both sides of the rock we again observe square niches, which served for the reception of beams. But what is of the greatest interest are the caves underneath the boulder, which form several cells separated from each other by walls. These are evidently the last remnants of an ancient Buddhist monastery. But the cells are filled with earth almost up to the ceiling, and it would be a grand thing if at some time they could be excavated. That this monastery was once larger is

Mon musicians, Kalatse

Ancient sculptures at Spadum above the deserted Monastery

Ancient Buddhist sculptures from Baltistan

Stone images at Dras

Sculptures at Sheh. Image of Maitreya, raised probably by King Nyimagon about 975 A.D.

Lamayuru Monastery. The ancient stronghold of the Bon religion

Spitug Monastery, built by King Bum Lde

Bragnaz Castle at Kalatse

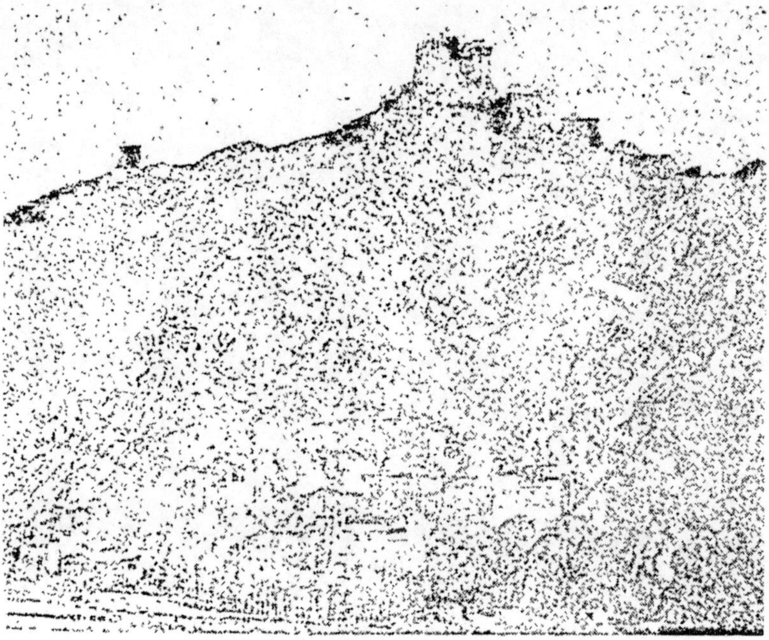

Namgyal Tsemo Hill at Leh with the village of Chubi, built by Trashi Namgyal about 1520 A.D.

The Mani Wall of King Deldan Namgyal at Leh

The Palace of Senge Namgyal in Leh from the

Village of Basgo, with ruins

View of Sheh. On the hill, ruins of the ancient capital Ladakh. at foot of hill, the modern castle of the Kings

New Palace of Stog, built by King Tsepal Dondrub Namgyal, about 1820 A.D.

:-King Sodnam Namgyal, grandson of Jigsmed Namgyal

Ruins of Custom House at Balukar

Kalatse Bridge, where Sukamir's hand was fastened to a pole as a warning

proved by the two niches for beams above it.

The life which once pulsed in this now deserted place was probably not very different from that in Indian monasteries of those days. That the monks wore the yellow robe is without doubt. But it is of the greatest interest that down to the present day the yellow robe is still worn by certain Lamaist sects now residing in Zangskar. I myself once saw two Zangskar Lamas who wore yellow robes. K. Marx makes the following remark with regard to the colour of the Lamas' dress in Tibet; "There is an error prevalent regarding the dress of Lamas, viz., that the dress of Lamas of the 'red' persuasion is red, and that of the 'yellow' persuasion, yellow. This is not so. The dress of both, the 'red' and 'yellow' Lamas, is red, with the exception of the one special order of the *Geldanpa*, who, to my knowledge, *only exist in Zangskar, whose dress is also yellow.* But Lamas of the 'red' persuasion also wear red caps and red scarfs round their waist, whilst in the case of the 'yellow' Lamas *these* and these *only* are yellow." The simplest explanation of the fact that in Zangskar alone the original Buddhist colour of the clerical robe has been preserved to the present day is probably that Zangskar was not affected by King *Lha chen ngorub's* command, viz., that all novices were to go to Central Tibet for study, and that here the original Buddhism lingered on for several more centuries before it was swallowed up by Lamaism.

Besides those described above, I also came across other remains of the ancient Mons in Zangskar. Near the village of Zangla there is a boulder by the roadside, one side of which is covered all over with pictures of pyramidal chaityas. These pictures are carved in the rock, and the lines are painted with red colour. At the village of Stongrdze I was taken to the last remains of the stupas and chaityas, which are still called *Mongyi mani*, mani of the Mons. Although not much was left of them, it could be seen that their original shape must have been like that of those pictured on the boulder at *Zangla*.

By the natives a number of ruined castles in Zangskar are called *Mongyi mkhar*, "castle of the Mons." This was said in particular of the following: *Drakar*, *Darkungtse*, near *Sanid*, and a fort near *Tsadar*. But the the most important fortification of the ancient Mons seems to have been the castle of *Spadum*, which was connected with the fortified village of *Ghor ghor* by a long masonry rampart. This rampart protected the fortification on one side, whilst on the other there was the river. This kind of fortification appeals to the sense of Europeans, because in this case we can understand a fortress offering a prolonged resistance, there being no danger that the water would run short. But it is difficult for us to understand why so many castles in this country were built on bare cliffs, in which case it remains a mystery how the besieged party supplied itself with water.

This is a *resume* of the principal items of interest which are known with regard to the Mons of Ladakh. Who would think, when he sees a low caste Mon of the present day, that he has before him a probable descendant of those ancient Buddhist missionaries, whose imposing works of art have hardly ever been excelled in Western Tibet?

SONG OF A MON MUSICIAN (*Lad. Songs*, No. L.)

The Tibetan Fiddle.

Do not think that my fiddle, called Trashi wanggyal,
Does not possess a great father !
If the divine wood of the pencil cedar
Is not its great father, what else ?

Do not think that my fiddle, called Trashi wanggyal,
Does not possess a little mother !
If the strings from the goat
Are not its little mother, what else ?

Do not think that my fiddle, called Trashi wanggyal
Does not possess any brothers !
If the ten fingers of my hand
Are not its brothers, what else ?

Do not think that my fiddle, called Trashi wanggyal,
Does not possess any friends !
If the sweet sounds of its own mouth
Are not its friends, what else ?

Refrain—
Shab shab ma zhig shab shab ma zhig,
Tse sang ma zhig sang mol.

3

The Migrations of the Dards

ALTHOUGH the Mons had, besides preaching the "law" founded villages and towns in desert Western Tibet, much arable ground remained, and this fact was now recognised by the Dards of Gilgit.

It is quite possible that the colonisation of Western Tibet by the Mons and Dards met with no opposition from the Tibetan nomads, because their interest lay in different directions; and, although a few irrigated plains were occupied by these Aryans, there remained ample pasture-ground for the flocks of the Tibetans. But it is possible that hostilities sprang up occasionally between the Dards and the Mons, and that the Mons were subdued in this struggle. Otherwise, it is hardly possible to explain why the position of the Mons became so much lower than that of the Dards.

Although no written historical records of the Dards of Western Tibet have as yet been found, we know a great deal more about them than we know of the Mons. This is principally due to the fact that a certain number of them have not yet lost their language, and have withstood the tide of Tibetan culture that has swept over them. There are two tribes of Dards still existing in the territories of the former Ladakhi kingdom who have preserved their original language : the Dards of Dras, and the Dards of Da. The most interesting of the two are the latter. Those of Dras became Mussulmans about three centuries ago, and, in consequence, most of their original customs and folklore have been stamped out. Those of Da have neither become Mohammedans nor have they accepted Lamaism wholeheartedly, and thus much of their originality has been preserved.

The Dards of Da have, indeed, a festival which is celebrated every third year, but occasionally oftener, when they try to forget for a few days that they have come under the sway of Tibetan and Dogra masters. For those few days they want to be Dards only, and in a long hymnal they sing of old Dard days. It is through this hymnal that we get some news of their past.

In the sixth of these hymns they give the names of all those colonies on the Indus which were founded by this special tribe of Dards; and the most eastern of them is *Rong chu rgyud*, a long way beyond Leh, in a district which we should hardly have ever suspected of having been Dard. On the relevant map all the present and former settlements of the Dards are shaded with lines. Those are marked entirely dark where the Dard language is still spoken. Those places which are claimed by the Dards of Da as having been founded by their forefathers on their emigration from Gilgit are marked with vertical lines. Those where I have discovered traces of the Dards, either in the form of ruined castles, deserted oases, or graves, are marked with horizontal lines.

From the map it becomes evident that the influence of the Dards on the development of Western Tibet must have been enormous, and we ask with astonishment how it is that they disappeared entirely from most parts of the country. Is the story of their fall known? Popular tradition tells us something of their last days; but their end was not everywhere the same. It is not likely that a nation whom Herodotus called the most warlike of all the Indians should have given in so easily, and there are tales current which speak of the stubborn resistance of the last Dards. Thus at *Nyerags* the following Samson-like story is told of the fall of those Dards : "The Dards were besieged in their castle (probably by Tibetans), and when their supplies of food and water came to an end they resolved to die together. So they all assembled in the central hall of the castle, and the oldest man pushed away the stone on which stood the central pillar supporting the roof, and the falling roof buried them all." A story of the Hanu Dards runs as follows : "The Tibetan kings, who considered the people of Hanu their subjects, ordered them to join the rest of the population in doing forced labour. The king was opposed by an old Dard, who told him that the Dards considered it beneath their dignity to be the slaves of a king. This old man was now selected to work all by himself in the presence of the king. But all means failed to make him do any work, and at last he was condemned to be immured. When the wall reached up to his neck he was asked once more if he was ready to work, but, as he still refused, the wall was closed." Still, the old man does not seem to have sacrificed his life in vain for his people; for an almost destroyed rock-inscription, a few miles above the Hanu gorge, is still shown as the edict of the king who released the Dards from forced labour. Unfortunately, the name of the king cannot be deciphered. There is still a proverb in use with regard to this incident : "You cannot force labour on a Dard, just as you cannot put a load on a dog!" To deprive the Dards of Hanu of their national feeling, the last Tibetan kings prohibited the use of the Dard language and posted spies to report every individual who spoke Dardi.

The disappearance of the Dards, at Kalatse for instance, seems to have taken place in an altogether peaceful manner, according to local tradition. All those Dards who lived between Kalatse and the little village of Skinding, moved down to Kalatse or up to Skinding, one after another, and were quite satisfied to be Tibetanised. Only in a few houses at Kalatse a prayer in Dardi is still rendered to the guardian spirit of the house on New Year's Day, because this deity is supposed to have not yet acquired a sufficient knowledge of Tibetan.

As regards the religion of the ancient Dards, it was probably the form of Buddhism which was prevalent in the days of emigration at Gilgit. The many stone images without date which are found all over Ladakh testify to this, and many of them show a particularly strong resemblance to those found about Gilgit (see *The Tribes of the Hindo Kush*). But Buddhism does not appear to have been very firmly rooted among them, and their old traditions were hardly given up for the sake of Buddhism. In the hymnal mentioned above we find a song of the origin of the world which probably contains their most ancient ideas with regard to that event. It is this :

How did the earth first grow ?
At first the earth grew on a lake.
What grew on the water ?
On the water grew a meadow.
What grew on the meadow ?
Three hills grew there.
What are the names of the three hills ?
The name of one hill is the "White Jewel Hill."
What is the name of another hill ?
The name of another hill is the "Red Jewel Hill."
What is the name of the one remaining hill ?
The name of the one remaining hill is the "Blue Jewel Hill."
What grew on the three hills ?
Three trees grew there.
What are the names of the three trees ?
The name of one tree is the "White Sandal Tree,"
The name of another is the "Blue Sandal Tree,"
The name of the one remaining tree is the "Red Sandal Tree."

What birds grew on the three trees ?
Three birds grew on the three trees.
What is the name of one bird ?
The name of one bird is "Wild Eagle."
What is the name of another bird ?
The name of another bird is "Barndoor Hen."
What is the name of the one remaining bird ?
The name of the one remaining bird is "Blackbird."

The three mountains and trees are possibly thought to exist one on top of the other, and thus to constitute the three worlds in correspondence to the land of the gods, of men, and of the water-spirits, of the Tibetan pre-Buddhist religion. Also the system of colours—white for heaven, red for earth, and blue for the lower world—is the same as that of the Tibetans. But in other respects the Dard system is different from the Tibetan system. Thus, according to the Tibetans, the earth is formed out of the body of a giant, whilst here it grows out of the water.

The Dards were great carvers on the rocks, and some of the drawings of animals are quite works of art (*see* Plates). But the drawings which are of the greatest interest to us are those which show the Dards in their original costumes. Such carvings I have discovered at Hunupata and at Kalatse. On the rocks of Hunupata the Dard women are represented as wearing long ungirded gowns and very high pointed caps, a costume which agrees exactly with the one still worn by the Dard women of Dras. The costume of the Dard men, represented on the same rock, has entirely disappeared, the reason being that at the time of the last Ladakhi kings certain types of dress were ordered to be worn by the whole male population.

On a rock near Kalatse, a Dard woman carrying a basket on her back is represented. Her headdress is considered by the present people of Kalatse to be identical with the headdress of the present women of Da, looking at it from the front. She wears her gown tucked up very high, as the women of Da do when working. On another rock at the same place is a picture of a man hunting antelopes. His headdress looks like a flat hat furnished with a tie for a tail. On other rocks near Kalatse men with something like flat hats on their heads can be seen.

From these carvings we may infer that the ancestors of the Dards at Hunupata belong to the same tribe as the Dards of Dras, and those of Kalatse to the Dards of Da.

In the *Tribes of Hindo Kush*, with regard to the Dards of Da the supposition is expressed that this tribe emigrated from Gilgit during the seventeenth century. It is of course possible that single families have emigrated as lately as that time. But the emigration of the tribe as a whole must have taken place at a much earlier date. The chief reasons for my belief are again of a philological nature. If the emigration had taken place during the seventeenth century, it could hardly be explained why the dialect of this particular tribe is so much at variance with the present Dard language at Gilgit; whilst the Dras dialect is still practically the same as the Gilgit dialect. The Dards of Da must have been without connection with the Dards of Gilgit for a very long time back, whilst the language areas of Dras and of Gilgit never seem to have been separated by speakers of other languages.

But the Dards of Da themselves may have given rise to the supposition of their late emigration. It is an ancient Dard custom to bury the dead. Now, the present Dards of Da, discovering the old burial-ground of their forefathers in a side valley near Da, jumped to the conclusion that their forefathers must have been Mussulmans, because they observed that their Mussulman neighbours always bury their dead. If the Dards had emigrated in Mussulman times, of course, the date of their emigration would be rather late.

Besides the custom of burial, the Dards are known for many more strange customs, the origin of which has not yet been explained satisfactorily. Thus they do not breed fowls, nor do they eat their eggs; the milk of cows is also not used by them, although they breed Dzos (the hybrid of the yak and common cow) to sell them to other people.

The question very naturally arises, whether the ancient Dards were illiterate or not. It is as yet very difficult to decide this question definitely. Those ancient inscriptions in Indian Brahmi and Kharoshthi characters of 200 B.C., which have been found at Kalatse, more likely belong to the times of the ancient Mons. However, in front of the ancient Dard castle at Kalatse, there is a short inscription in a later form of Indian character. This may be a document of the civilisation of those Dards.

But more than literature the Dards enjoyed sports; and in many places, where their language has become extinct, the game of polo which they introduced has survived to the present day. This game, which was played by the ancient Persians, as we know from their monuments, fell into disuse. The Dards, however, kept it up. In the more western parts of Western Tibet it is known better than in the eastern parts. The most famous polo-ground in Ladakh has been that of Chigtan, about which a song exists. But in Baltistan the game is still played in the old ceremonial style, which reminds us of European mediaeval tournaments. Rock-carvings seem to tell also of other entirely forgotten sports—for instance, standing on the backs of bulls, and shooting arrows whilst they were charging, and horse baiting. But the commonest sport was hunting, and not only do the rock-carvings refer to it, but in an ancient song a hunting scene, with bow and arrow, which took place at Gilgit on the occasion of a dance, is described in full.

At Brushal and Gilgit
One hundred youths appear.

In the fertile village of Satsil
One hundred maids appear.
They form a great assembly at Gilgit;
The lion-king of Gilgit appears at the head of the dancers.
Then all you girls, twirl your hands, to greet us !
All you boys, clap your hands, to greet us !
Hurrah for love ! Well done, hallo !
On the Ambir pass it makes "tarag" !
Take the arrow, then the bow, then the arrow-shafts and the heads,
Oh boy that art clever at hiding !...
Then, oh boy, clever at climbing;
Then, oh boy, who art clever at imitating the antelope's cry;
Then, oh boy, who art clever at getting out of sight,
There the ibex can be seen, the ibex can be seen in a herd !
Now take the arrow, oh boy;
Now take the bow, oh boy;
Then take the arrow-shafts and heads,
Oh boy that art clever at driving them together;
Oh boy that art clever at driving them to heaps;
Thou that art clever at singling out the best;
Thou that art clever at shooting them!
Offerings of flour, butter, milk, and water,
Must now be brought ! Honour to thee, oh God !
Now cut the flesh with a sharp knife;
Roasted meat must be offered !
Cut it to pieces !
Give a mouthful to each of one hundred boys !
They will carry the meat in their pockets of leather;
They will give some to father and mother, oh boy !
They will make presents of it to one hundred girls, oh boy !
Now we have come to happiness and abundance, oh boy !

4

Chinese Records of Western Tibet, say 640-760 A.D.

DURING the seventh and eighth centuries several Chinese Buddhists made pilgrimages to the famous Buddhist shrines of North India. The Chinese are noted for their historical and geographical acumen, a faculty which the Indians do not possess. Thus the diaries kept by the Chinese pilgrims on their Indian tours are of the highest value for the study of ancient Indian geography and archaeology. Unfortunately, none of these pilgrims apparently passed through Western Tibet on their way from China to India, and thus we have to be satisfied with a few references to our territories which were made by them when they arrived in the neighbourhood of Western Tibet.

It was believed for some time that one of the earliest of them, *Fa Hian*, say 400 A.D., had passed through our country, because the description he gives of the kingdom of *Kie cha* in his diary might actually pass for a description of Ladakh. Therefore, General Sir Alexander Cunningham accepted *Kie cha* as the Chinese rendering of some ancient name of Ladakh; and Legge identified *Kie cha* with Skardo in Baltistan. Modern scholars, in particular Dr M. A. Stein, have proved, however, that *Kie cha* stands for Kashgar, in Turkestan.

Hiuen Tsang went on his pilgrimage about 640 A.D. He spent two years in Kashmir, and there seems to have heard people occasionally mention the neighbouring districts of Western Tibet. Thus, he gives a short description of the road to Baltistan, which he calls *Po-lu-lo* (the Chinese rendering of the ancient name *Bolor* of that country). He says: "Since the erection of this statue (of Maitreya in the streamlet *Tha-li-lo*, the modern *Darel*, near a great monastery) the law has spread considerably to the east. To the east of this point, traversing the hills and the valleys, ascending the *Sin-tou* (Indus), crossing flying bridges, logs of timber, precipices, and marshes, and proceeding in all 500 *li*, you come to the country of *Po-lu-lo*." This description shows that in those days travelling in the Western Himalayas was not particularly pleasant, and difficulties and obstacles only encountered now on branch roads were then the ordinary features of the main road.

There must have been some reason why the pilgrim spent such a comparatively long time in Kashmir, *Kia-shi-mi-lo*, as he calls it, and Dr Stein has the following note on the point: "With all due respect for the spiritual fervour of the pilgrim and the excellence of his Kashmirian preceptors, it is difficult to suppress the surmise that the material attractions of the valley had something to do with his long stay. The cool air of Kashmir, the northern aspect of its scenery and products, have at all times exercised their powerful charm over those visitors who, themselves born in colder climes, have come to the valley from the heat and dust of the Indian plains."

With regard to the situation of *Po-lu-lo* (Baltistan), *Hiuen Tsang* makes the remark that it is found south of *Pho-mi-lo*, the Pamir.

General Cunningham also believed that *Hiuen Tsang* was speaking of Western Tibet under the name of *Mo-lo-pho*, which name corresponds to the ordinary name *Mar yul* of the Ladakhi kingdom (*Marpa*=a man of *Mar yul*). He based his opinion on *Hiuen Tsang's* remark that *Mo-lo-pho* was situated on the other side of the mountains when travelling from *Kiu-lu-to* (Kulu), and on the fact that *San-pho-ho* is given as another name of *Mo-lo-pho*; and the word *San-pho-ho* reminded Cunningham of the Tibetan name of the Indus (*tsangpho*= river). But since his days *Mo-lo-pho* has been looked for in other districts, and one of the most recent attempts at identifying it is that with *Malva*, in India, by Vincent Smith. As this is evidently a failure, the question of the situation of *Mo-lo-pho* is still open.

Further information respecting Western Tibet, from Chinese

sources, is contained in the annals of the Tang dynasty. Those were the days when the Chinese pushed on towards the West with a great amount of energy.

During the time of the Chinese progress in the far West, Turkestan, Western Tibet, and Kashmir became part of the celestial empire. These conquests took place during the first part of the eighth century. From the Chinese annals we learn that "the first embassy from Kashmir arrived at the Imperial Court in or shortly after A.D. 713. In the year 720 *Tchen-tho-lo-pi-li*, ruler of Kashmir, the *Chandrapida* of the Kashmir chronicles, was accorded by imperial decree the title of king."[1] It is of some interest to notice that the Kashmir book of chronicles, the famous Rajatarangini, does not make the least mention of the subjugation of Kashmir by China, nor does it refer to the annual tribute that had to be sent to China. The Kashmir policy of those days seems to have been one of yielding to the strong and bullying the weak. It looks as if the Kashmir troops had not offered much resistance to the Chinese, and as if the Kashmir king had early sought the friendship of the Chinese. He was apparently quite satisfied with his recognition as a vassal king. It was different with Western Tibet. Although the land was split up into a great number of petty principalities, as will be shown more fully in the next chapter, the Tibetans were ready to fight; and the state which offered the most serious obstacle to the progress of the Chinese was Baltistan. Several expeditions became necessary against *Po-liu*, as Baltistan was then called, and the first of them took place some time between 736 and 747.

With a sufficient army at one's disposal, it could not have been very difficult to gain victory over one or other of the numerous little kingdoms between Leh and Kashmir which were continually at war with each other; and this fact was recognised by the next Kashmir king, *Lalitaditya*, or *Muktapida*, the *Mou-to-pi* of the Chinese annals. He boasted of his victories over the Tibetans, and, although his expeditions against them were mere raids for the sake of plunder, he pretended he had been engaged in serious operations.

1. Quoted from Dr M.A. Stein's *Ancient Geography of Kashmir*.

He sent an envoy called *Ou-li-to* to the Chinese court. This man was to report the victories of his master over the Tibetans, and at the same time to solicit the establishment of a camp of Chinese troops by the banks of the lake *Mo-ho-to-mo-loung* (*Mahapadma* or *Volur* lake). The Kashmir king offered to provide all necessary supplies for an auxiliary force of 200,000 men. But the "Divine Khan" found it more convenient to content himself with issuing decrees for the sumptuous entertainment of the ambassador and for the recognition of *Muktapida* under the title of king. "Since that time the relations of Kashmir with the celestial empire and the payment of tribute from the former is said to have continued to this day."[1]

Of particular interest to us is that the Chinese annals speak of "Great and Little Poliu"; from this we infer that the names of "Great and Little Tibet" were known in those ancient days, Baltistan in particular being called "Little Tibet." This name is found often in the works of the later Kashmir historians.

The political relations between China and the northern kingdoms of India seem to have ceased soon after the time of *Ou-khong*, the Chinese pilgrim, of whom we shall now speak. This was probably due to the Chinese power under the later Tang gradually losing ground in Central Asia before the Uigurs and Tibetans.

Ou-khong reached Kashmir in 759 A.D., and spent a considerable time in the country. His remarks concerning two of the three roads leading into Kashmir are of some interest in relation to Western Tibet. Dr Stein gives his information in the following words : "In the east a road leads into *Thou-fan*, or Tibet; in the north there is a road which reaches into *Po-liu*, or Baltistan; the road which starts from the 'western gate' goes to *Khien-tho-lo*, or Gandhara. We have here a clear enough description of the great routes through the mountains which since ancient times have formed the main lines of communication between the valley and the outer world. The road to *Thou-fan* corresponds undoubtedly to the present route over the Zoji-la to Ladakh and hence to Tibet. The road to Poliu is

1. Quoted from Dr M.A. Stein's *Ancient Geography of Kashmir*.

represented by the present 'Gilgit Road,' leading into the upper Kishanganga valley and thence to Skardo on the Indus. The third route is by the Baramulla gorge."

The Chinese pilgrims after *Ou-khong* are of little importance and need not be mentioned.

From the Chinese sources we hear of the first great war which raged in Western Tibet, and although the information is both vague and scanty, we can well imagine that the country was shaken to its very foundations by this continual warfare. It will be fitting here to cite an ancient "call to arms" as we find it in the Kesar epic, which was probably composed after the model of a real "call to arms" of bygone days. The women are also called to battle, and Tibetan folklore speaks of several women who were able to fight.

> Thou host of the heavens, come to the fight,
> And Wangpo *Gyabzkin* be at thy head !
> Thou host of the earth, come to the fight,
> And Mother *Skyabdun* be at thy head !
> Thou host of the waters, come to the fight,
> And Water-king *Ljogpo* be at thy head !
> At the head of the heroes, of Ling, *Palle* must stride ;
> At the head of the women of Ling, *Astag* must ride !
> At the head of the Lamas of Ling, *Tsegu* must ride ;
> At the head of the Mons of Ling, *Penog* must stride !
> At the head of the smiths of Ling, *Karog* shall ride ;
> At the head of the *Bhedos* of Ling, *Kangrings* shall stride !
> You boys who know how to use the sling, go the to war ;
> You girls who know how to use the spindle, go to the war !
> Whoever can provide for himself, let him do so ;
> Whoever cannot, let him be provided for at the castle of Ling !
> Whoever has a horse of his own, let him bring it ;
> Whoever has none, let him get one at the castle of Ling !
> March off then towards the land of Hor,
> And the king shall march in front of you all !

5

The Time of the Tibeto-Dard Kingdoms, about 500-1000 A.D.

We now meet with the first Tibetan historical records. They are of two kinds : there are records on rocks and records on paper. With regard to the political state of the country about 950 A.D. the chronicles of Ladakh make the following remarks : "At, that time Upper Ladakh was held by the descendants of Gesar (Kesar), whilst Lower Ladakh was split up into various independent principalities."

As we have shown in the previous chapters, the irrigable valleys of Western Tibet had been brought under cultivation by the Aryan tribes of the Mons and Dards, and the latter especially exhibited an extraordinary skill in the construction of water courses along almost inaccessible cliffs. The products of the fields were as welcome to the Tibetan nomads as were the produce of the flocks to the Dard peasants, and the lively barter which took place between the two tribes apparently led to many matrimonial "bargains" as well, and so a race grew up which combined the agriculturalist and the nomad. What is beautiful, to our taste, in the features of the present West Tibetans is due to their half-Dard origin; and what is not, to their half-Tibetan parentage. The growth of villages in many parts of the country led to the formation of chieftainships, or, in other words, to the state of things we find in 950 A D.

From local tradition and inscriptions it is possible to gather some scanty information about the various states which were in existence before the time of the Central Tibetan dynasty. At Leh their reigned a dynasty of kings who derived their origin from the mythical king *Kesar*; at Saspola people tell of a king *Bandel*, the constructor of the ancient fort *Alchi kargog*. At Kalatse there was a dynasty of Dard kings whose fort was built on the bank of the Indus, and whose last members were called *Shirima*, *Gya shin*, and (probably) *Tri od*, according to inscriptions. It apparently came to an end between 1150-1200 A.D. At Lamayuru the paramount power seems to have been a monastery. The villages of *Da* and *Garkunu* were ruled by *magspons*, or "dukes," just as the Baltis were; but these villages have always been independent of Baltistan. At *Kartse*, near Kargil, reigned a dynasty of chiefs who called themselves *Tri rgyal*, according to an inscription; these altered their title into *Tri Sultan*, after they became Mussulmans. This dynasty lasted down to the time of the Dogra war, but is extinct now; the only dynasty of petty chiefs whose representatives are still alive is the line of the *Jobo rjes* of Chigtan, who altered their title to *Purig Sultan*, after they became Mohammedans. This dynasty possesses a written chronicle which goes back to the days when its ancestors had not yet left Gilgit. It is a genuine Dard dynasty.

Local tradition at Kalatse tells of the general state of things in those days. There was continual warfare between the many petty kings; particularly difficult were the harvest seasons. When the fruit of the field was being cut, half of the men of the village had to be on guard with bow and arrow, whilst the other half reaped. Suddenly the men of the village of *Tagmachig* would turn up in full armour and try to carry off the whole harvest, if possible. A few days after the young men of Kalatse would start on a raid to Tagmachig, to pay these people back in their own coin.

It is astonishing to find that in those unsafe times trade was carried on through Western Tibet, apparently between India and Yarkand. There are the ruins of an ancient fortified custom-house, called *Balutkar*, not far from Kalatse This custom-house guarded an ancient bridge across the Indus, and the custom-officer who was stationed there had the title *mdo gtsong gtso*, "Lord of the trade in the lower valley." As many ancient beads have been found at this site, it is believed that the tax had to be paid in kind and not in money, for not a single coin has as yet been discovered there. The ancient orthography employed in the inscription and other circumstances make it

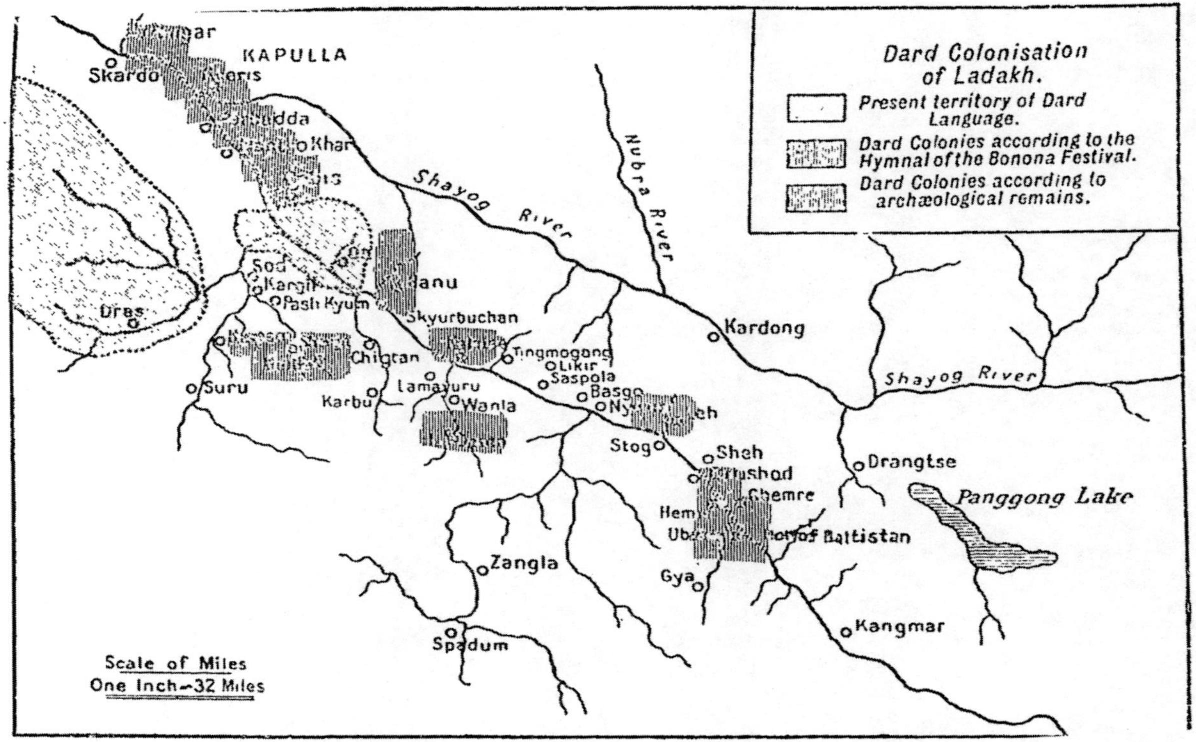
Dard Colonisation of Ladakh.
Present territory of Dard Language.
Dard Colonies according to the Hymnal of the Bonona Festival.
Dard Colonies according to archæological remains.
KAPULLA
Skardo
Khar
Shayog River
Nubra River
Sod
Kargil
Pash Kyum
Dras
Skyurbuchan
Chigtan
Tingmogang
Likir
Saspola
Basgo
Kardong
Suru
Karbu
Lamayuru
Wanla
Stog
Sheh
Chemre
Hem
Baltistan
Drangtse
Panggong Lake
Zangla
Gya
Kangmar
Spadum
Scale of Miles
One Inch—32 Miles

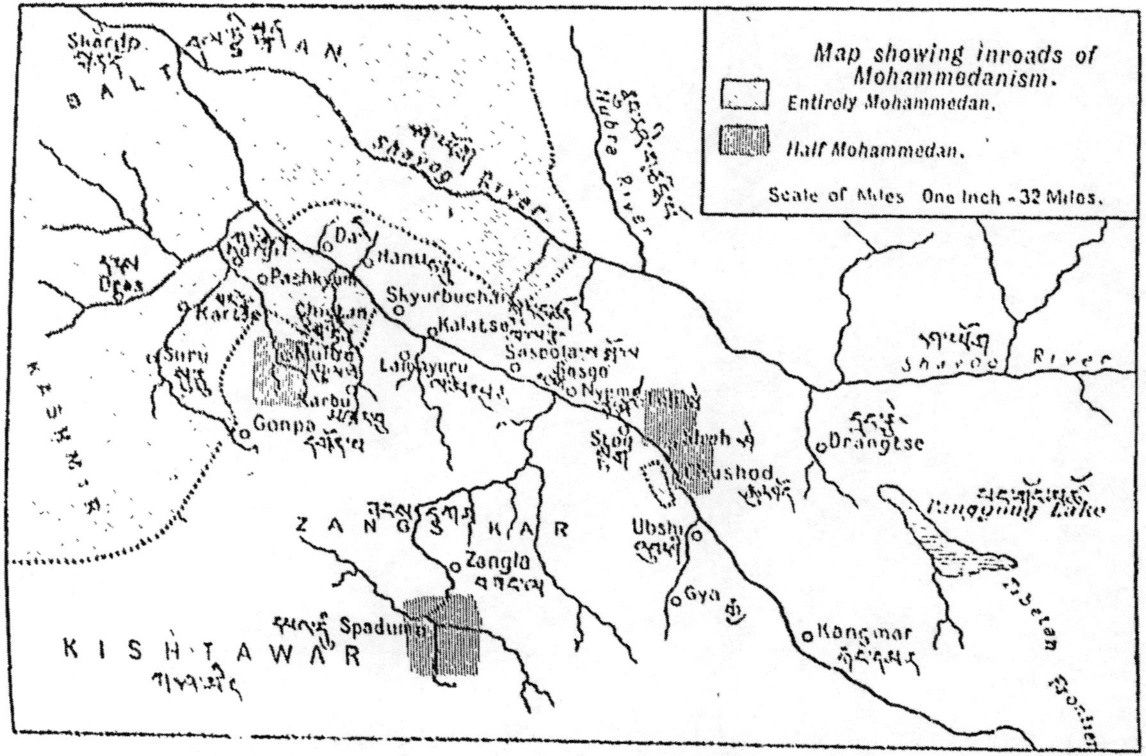
Map showing inroads of Mohammedanism.
Entirely Mohammedan.
Half Mohammedan.
Scale of Miles One Inch - 32 Miles.
Shardo
BALTISTAN.
Shayog River
Nubra River
Shayog River
Dras
Kartse
Suru
Dah
Hanu
Pashkyum
Skyurbuchan
Chiktan
Kalatse
Mulbe
Lamayuru
Saspola
Basgo
Karbu
Gonpa
Stog
Chushod
Drangtse
Pangong Lake
Ubshi
Gya
Kangmar
Tibetan Frontier
ZANGSKAR
Zangla
Spadum
KISHTAWAR
KASHMIR

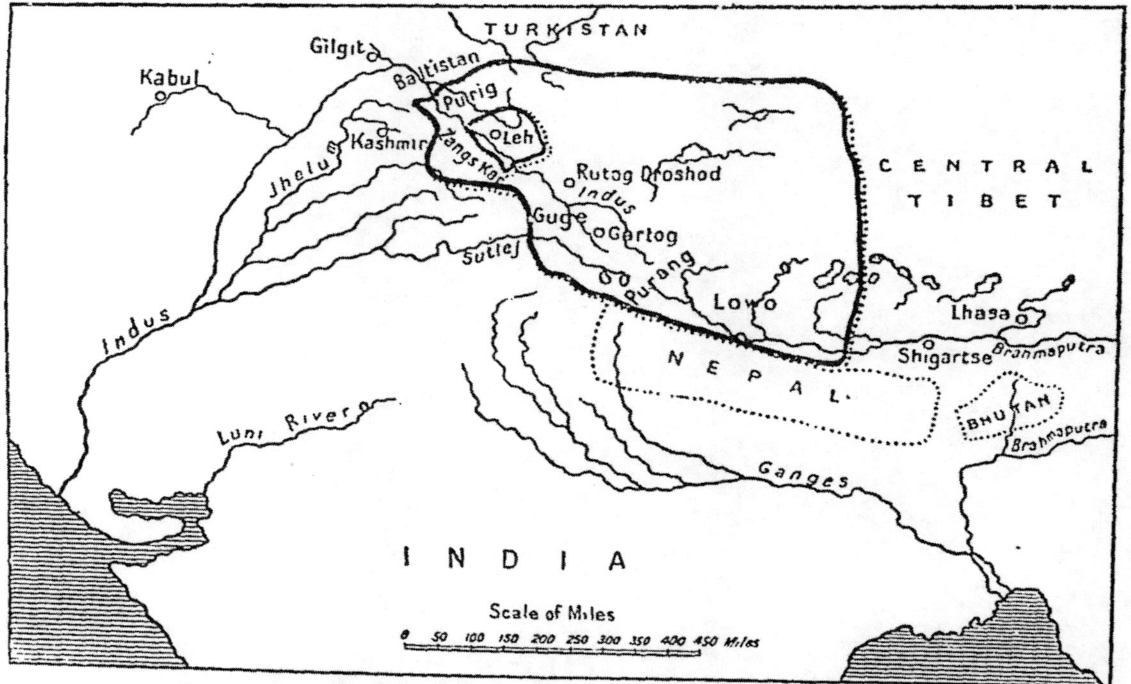

The Empire of King Tsewang Rnam Rgyal I., and that of King Jamyang Rnam Rgyal., about 1560 and 1600 A.D.

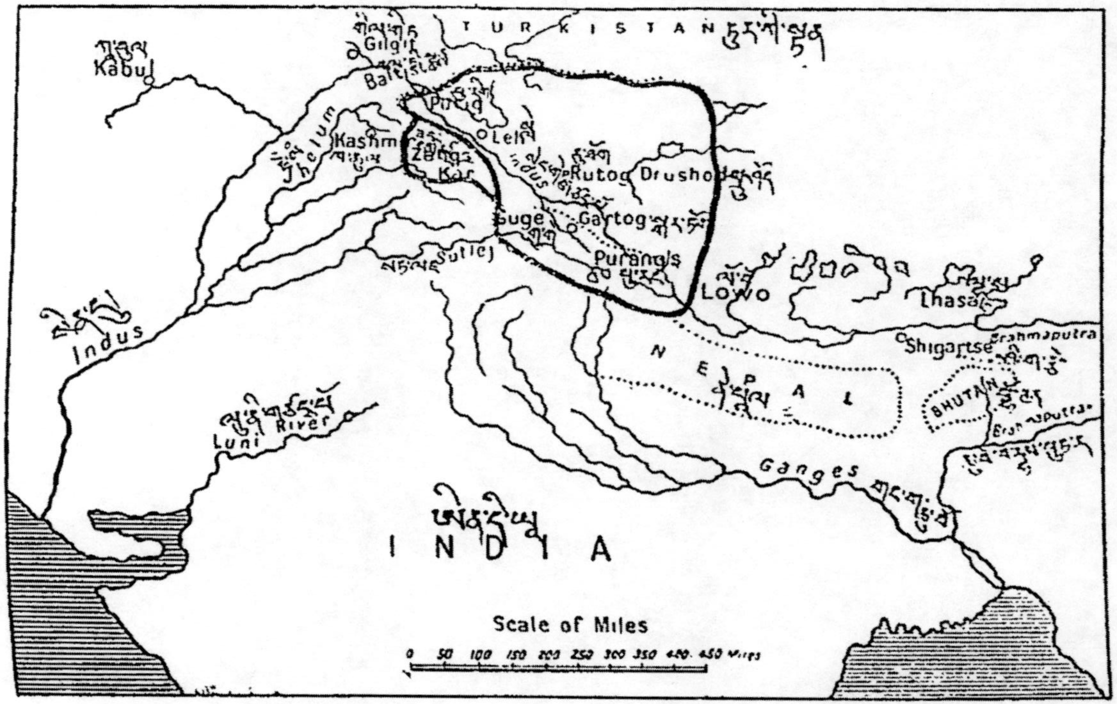

The Empire of King Nyimagon with its three Divisions: about 975-1000 A.D.

probable that the inscription was carved on the rock below the castle about 800-1000 A.D., more probably under the Tibetan king *Tri shrong de tsan*.

There are two ancient Central Tibetan kings, *Mu tri tsanpo* and *Tri shrong de tsan*, who claim to have conquered Western Tibet during this period.

Turning to the religious condition of the country, we remark that in those days there were apparently two religions co-existent in Western Tibet : Buddhism and Bonchos.

Buddhism had entered the country by two channels : the ancient Mons had brought it from India, and the Dards from Gilgit. During this period Buddhism was strengthened by the emigration of many Buddhist monks from Kashmir. Concerning this emigration there exist written records, and one of them is the Tibetan work *Padma bka btang*. The emigration did not take place in consequence of severe persecution : it had its origin in the general decline from Buddhism in Kashmir, which deprived the monks of their sources of revenue. The time when this emigration took place can be roughly fixed at about 600-1000 A.D. When Hiuen Tsang visited Kashmir, he found "the mass of the population addicted to the *devas*, and the monasteries few and partly deserted." If *Ou khong's* account is correct, the Buddhism of Kashmir looked a little more hopeful at the time of his visit; but after the destruction of the famous monastery of Nalanda in the ninth century it was fast losing ground. The most famous among the pupils of the Kashmir Buddhists who settled in Ladakh was *Lotsava Rinchen bzangpo*. He lived in the year 954 according to Schlagintweit. According to the Tibetan historical work mentioned above, the Kashmiri monks first settled at *Sanid* in Zangskar, and built the *Kanika* monastery.[1] When they had finished painting the pictures some paint remained, and to make use of it they decided to build another monastery at *Sumda* in *Piling*, and a third at *Alchi*. The fourth given in the record is the *Manggyu* monastery. These monasteries can be easily distinguished from the

1. It is remarkable that the monks of this monastery wear the red garb. This shows that the yellow robe of such Zangskar monasteries as, for instance, Gargya, was not introduced by the Kashmir monks.

rest of the Ladakhi monasteries, their special marks being the following : the door beams and lintels are very thick and ornamented all over with mythological wood-carvings. Of special interest are the galleries, if they have been preserved, as, for instance, at Alchi, with their trefoiled arches in genuine Kashmir style. The large hall is decorated with paintings only : if there are images in it nowadays they are later additions. These paintings represent Buddhist saints, often nude and in a standing position, and are sometimes painted on oval medallions which rise a little above the surface of the wall. Although only four monasteries are mentioned in the Tibetan book, several more have been built by Kashmiri emigrants, because in at least two more ruined monasteries K. Marx was able to point out the characteristics given above. One he discovered at Basgo and another at Chigtan. I have visited the latter and discovered in the hall, besides a Tibetan inscription by the chiefs of Chigtan, a Sanskrit inscription in Kashmir Sarada characters. The fact that by these monks the Sarada characters were used seems to provide a clue to the nature of the well-known stone images at Dras. General Cunningham found on one of them an inscription in Kashmir Sarada characters, and read the word *Maitreyan* among others. As, however, the principal figure represented in his opinion a woman, he did not know what to make of it. According to the judgement of the Ladakhis, the figure is not a woman, but a plain Maitreya, and in these sculptures we probably have a monument of the introduction of Buddhist art from Kashmir.

The religion of the Tibetan part of the population was from time immemorial of *Bon chos*. Although without a systematised religion for centuries, the contact with Buddhism taught the advisability of systematising the *Bon chos* and accepting certain forms from Buddhism. Thus lists of the water-spirits (*klu*) and other spirits were drawn up and monasteries founded. I am told that in some parts of Tibet *Bonpo* monasteries are still in existence. The most famous *Bonpo* monastery of Ladakh, according to popular tradition, was the *Yungdrung* monastery (now called *Lamayuru* or *Yuru*). It was called after the *svastika* (in Tibetan *yungdrung*), one of the symbols of the *Bon chos*, as well as of Buddhism and many other religions.

In the folklore of Western Tibet much of the unsystematised *Bon chos* seems to have been preserved, and the religious system of West Tibetan folklore has been drawn up by me under the name of *gLing chos*. The main features of this religion are the following :—The world consists of three great realms : the land of the gods, or heaven, which is of white colour; the land of men, or the earth, of red colour; and the land of the water-spirits, or lower world, of blue colour. There is a king reigning in heaven as well as in the under-world, but the greatest in power on the earth is the "earth-mother." There is a huge tree, the tree of the world, growing through all the three realms. It has its roots in the under-world and its highest branches in heaven. The king of heaven is asked to send one of his sons as king to the earth, and around the story of the mission of the youngest son of the king of heaven to the earth the national epic of Tibet in general, and Western Tibet in particular, has grown up.

Different from the national epics of other nations, the Tibetan national epic has not been preserved in one single version. Almost every village of Western Tibet has a version of its own which generally differs much from the version of the next village. But there is a version in existence which we may call the "official version." Lamaism took hold of this famous topic, and a poem was composed in which the ancient pre-Buddhist religious system was reconciled with Buddhism. This poem has, however, not achieved any popularity in Western Tibet. Here people prefer to listen to the village bard, when he sings to them the ancient songs, quaintly intermingled with passages in prose. The following is an abstract giving the main drift of the national epic :—

I. The forefather sows some seed, and a huge tree grows, from which a harvest of much fruit is obtained. The fruit is stored in a barn, and many worms come out of it. They eat up each other, until only one big worm remains. This changes into a boy, who marries eighteen girls, from whom the eighteen Agus (the heroes of the epic) are born. Then the boy kills a giant and builds the world out of his flesh and bones, in particular the castle of *Ling*. The Agus go to a very distant castle, from which they rob the treasures and store them up at Ling.

II. The king of heaven is assisted by one of the Agus when fighting the devil, and the Agu is allowed to ask a boon. He asks that one of the sons of the king of heaven may be sent to the earth as king. The youngest, *Dongrub*, is sent. He dies in heaven and is re-born on earth to a woman who had swallowed him in the form of a hailstone. Although he is the glorious King Kesar of Ling, he often exchanges his glorious appearance for a very poor outside, and also makes himself invisible. The traitor among the Agus makes some unsuccessful attempts to kill him.

III. Kesar is to be married to the maiden *Bruguma,* but her parents object to give him their daughter on account of his beggarly appearance. He has to accomplish several impossible tasks : peeling the skin off a huge yak who stretches from one hill to another, and cutting a wing off the sun-bird. He succeeds, and is accepted as son-in-law.

IV. The King of China becomes ill, and Kesar alone is able to heal him. The road to China is very difficult to find; besides, there are obstacles of many kinds, water, hills, snowstorms, ice, stones flying about in the air, male and female ogres. All are overcome, and the King of China is healed. The daughter of the king runs away with Kesar. As, however, the treasures of the king are carried off by the couple, Kesar is followed and thrown into a pit with three dragons. Kesar escapes in the shape of a fly, and goes to Ling with his new bride. Meanwhile the traitor among the Agus has seized the castle and turned out Bruguma. The traitor as well as the King of China are punished, and Kesar lives happily with his two wives.

V. Kesar goes to the North to conquer the giants of the North. Bruguma, who wants to accompany him, is sent back. After many difficulties Kesar arrives before the giant's castle, but does not find the giant at home. The giant's wife takes him in, and both have a happy time together. The giant's approach is indicated by an earthquake, and Kesar is hid by the lady in a hole underneath the ground. Although the giant smells at once the presence of a human being, he is pacified by his wife and induced to go to sleep. When he is fast asleep, Kesar is brought out of the hole and kills the giant.

VI. Whilst Kesar was away, the King of Hor had overrun

the land of Ling and stolen Bruguma. A message is carried to Kesar by storks, and he starts to save her. In the land of Hor he takes service at a smith's, and learns the trade. With the help of an iron rope made with the assistance of the smith, Kesar ascends the castle of Hor and kills the king in a wrestling contest. Bruguma, who is not quite without fault in the affair, is punished, and then both live happily together at the Ling castle.

Although there are many general features in the epic which remind us of Aryan and European myths, the groundwork of the sagas is apparently of Indo-Chinese origin, as almost the same tales are found in Chinese folklore. When, however, the similarity of minor features of the sagas with European and Indian tales is very great, we may suspect that in such cases the influence of the Mon and Dard colonies on this ancient literature makes itself felt.

I imagine that about the year 1000 A.D. the popularity of the Kesar saga was very great Personal names were taken from the saga. The dynasty of the ancient kings of Leh called itself after Kesar; at Kalatse the name of *rGya zhin* (the name of Kesar's heavenly father) occurs not only in a king's name but also in the names of other men, as is proved by rock-inscriptions. Also the name of the ancient castle at *Spadum* contains the same word. It was called *Spa dum rgya zhin pholad sku mkhar*.

I add a poem taken from the Kesar cycle (*Ladakhi Songs*, No. XXVII.).

BRUGUMA'S FAREWELL TO KESAR.

Oh, my clever king !
When thou goest to the upper land of the gods,
And seest all the fairies of heaven,
Then do not forget thy wife from the land of men !

Oh, my wise lord !
When thou goest to the upper land of the gods,
And seest all the beauties among the fairies,
Then do not reject Bruguma from the land of men !

Oh, my clever king !
When thou goest to the lower land of the nixes,
And seest all the lady-nixes of it,
Then do not forget thy wife from the land of men !

Oh, my wise lord !
When thou goest to the lower land of the nixes,
And seest all the beauties among its ladies,
Then do not reject thy helpmate from the land of men !

6

The Inauguration of the Central Tibetan Dynasty and its First Kings, about 900-1400 A.D.

N most inscriptions the Ladakhi kings call themselves "des-ndants of Nya tri tsanpo" (*gNya khri btsanpo*), the first king Tibet, whose date is about 200 or 300 B.C. But, although ese kings are very proud of belonging to the family of the eat kings of Tibet, they do not wish to be reminded of the ct that their special ancestor, after whom their dynasty branch-off from the Central Tibetan dynasty, was *Langdarma*, famous "Julian the Apostate" of Buddhism. Although Bud-ism had been introduced into Central Tibet about 400 A.D., did not become a great religion until King *Shrong tsan sgam-*, about 629 A.D., openly accepted it and used his influence to it spread over the whole of Tibet. Still, for about two more nturies, it had to fight for its existence, as the adherents of the cient *Bon chos* of Tibet were not willing to give up their ional creed for one introduced from a foreign country.

About 900 A.D the hope of the friends of the *Bon chos* was ntred in Prince *Langdarma*. Although Langdarma was er than his brother *Ralpachan*, he was excluded from the cession on the ground that he was inimical to Buddhism. wever, he got his chance when his brother was strangled by enemies of Buddhism. His first measure was to deprive monasteries of the conditions of tenure, and, in consequence this, many Indian pandits left Tibet. But the king found these had not sufficient effect, and he began to persecute ldhism openly. He was not quite without humour in his anger. Half of the many Buddhist monks had to become butchers, and the other half hunters. Whoever did not show a liking for his new profession was decapitated. But when Langdarma thought that he had succeeded in annihilating Buddhism, the snake which he thought he had crushed bit him. A Buddhist hermit put on a robe, black on the outside and white inside, because only black clothing (the colour of the *Bon chos*) was allowed to be worn in those days. But underneath his coat he kept a bow and arrow in readiness. He approached the king, as if he were a suppliant, and threw himself down on the floor. When Langdarma walked up to him, he suddenly rose and shot the king through his heart. Then, in order not to be recognised by those who had seen him enter in black, he put on his dress with the white outside and escaped.

This Langdarma is the special ancestor of the Western Tibetan kings. There is still an interesting reminiscence of Langdarma in the mode of dressing the hair of the Laḍakhi ex-kings. They wear long hair to cover the middle part of the head. People say that Langdarma had to wear his hair in this fashion to cover two horns, each an inch long, which grew out of his head. These horns proved that Langdarma was a devil in his role of "Julian the Apostate" of Buddhism. But the idea of his having horns may have been suggested by the first part of his name, which means "ox."

We are now entering the domain of Western Tibetan historiography, which, though not of classical value, as K. Marx justly remarks, is of the greatest importance for the student of history. Although it does not enable us to fix exact dates for the Ladakhi kings, it enables us to fix approximate dates with a great amount of certainty. It forms the backbone of the following outline of history, and quotations or information from it will always be marked thus [——]. Fortunately, we are able in many cases to enlarge on it, as documents on stone and paper will become more and more plentiful as we proceed.

[Langdarma had a legitimate son from the lesser queen, called *Odshrung* (about 925-950); but there was also an illegitimate son of the great queen, called *Yumstan*, and it was the latter who seized the government of Central Tibet.]

[Odshrung's son was *Ldepal kortsan* (*Lde dpal khor btsan*), about 950-975.]

[Ldepal kortsan had two sons—*Skyid lde nyima gon* (about 975-1000) and Trashi tsegspal. Both were robbed of all their possessions in Central Tibet by Yumstan, and fled to Western Tibet (called *Ngaris* in those days). Trashi tsegspal became king of the most eastern portion of Western Tibet, called Yarlung. But Skyid lde nyima gon conquered Western Tibet completely, although at the outset his army numbered only 300 horsemen.

On his way to Western Tibet he was once in such straitened circumstances that he had nothing to eat but eggs and fish. Now, his servants brought him this dish covered with a large napkin. From this it has come to be a custom with the kings of Tibet to use the so-called giant's napkin, which custom is still observed by the kings of Ladakh.]

The Dard people of Garkunu sing a song of King *Nyima gon* (which means something like "Sun-lord") and his son *Zlaba gon* (which means something like "Moon-lord"). According to this song Zlaba gon is killed by a Lama. Although I do not believe that Nyima gon had a son Zlaba gon, I presume that the Dard people, who were conquered by Nyima gon, knew that he was a descendant of Langdarma, who had been murdered by a Lama, and later on mixed up his forefather and son. But a song like this is one of the most certain proofs that the whole of Western Tibet was actually conquered by this king.

[The principal towns and castles said to have been built by Nyima gon are : Karmar in Rutog in the horse-year; Tseshogyari (not known) in the sheepyear;[1] several villages in Dam and Lag (probably in the Upper Sutlej valley), and Nyizungs in Purang, from which place he also obtained his wife.]

1. As these are the first dates given in the West Tibetan chronicles, it will be in place to say a few words about Tibetan chronology. The Tibetans as well as the Chinese have cycles of sixty years, which are differentiated by numbers. The first Tibetan cycle begins with the year 1027 A.D. (1026, according to Waddell). This great cycle of sixty years contains smaller cycles of twelve years each, the single years of which are named after twelve animals. To be able to distinguish *(Contd.)*

He is also, apparently, the king who ordered the principal sculptures at Sheh, which are nowadays known as *Sman la*, to be executed. In an inscription he says that he had them made for the religious benefit of the *Tsanpo* (the dynastical name of his father and ancestors), and of all the people of *Ngaris* (Western Tibet). This shows that already in this generation Langdarma's opposition to Buddhism had disappeared.

[*Lha chen palgyi gon*, about 1000-1025. Nyima gon had three sons, among whom he divided his kingdom. But it seems to have been understood that the younger brothers were in some degree of vassalage under their elder brother; for the kings of Leh continually claimed authority over the entire kingdom of Nyima gon.

Lha chen palgyi gon, the eldest, received Ladakh proper, from the Zoji Pass to Rutog and the goldmine of Gog. The name *Gog* is probably used in error for *Grog*, pronounced Dog, the *Thog* of the maps, east of Rutog. His portion was not only the largest, but certainly the most beautiful part of the empire.

Trashis gon, the second, received a long and narrow strip of country along the northern slope of the Himalayas, of which Purang and Guge are the best-known provinces.

Lde tsug gon, the youngest, received the southern provinces of the kingdom, of which Zangskar, Lahoul, and Spiti are best known. His portion was the smallest.]

Nothing is known about Trashis gon's descendants. Of Lde tsug gon's descendants eight generations are known. This line of kings has become famous through its connection with

(*Contd.*)

between the same animal years within the cycle of sixty, the animal's names are coupled with the names of the Tibetan five elements. Thus a date is complete if the following is given : 1. The number of the great cycle; 2. the animal of the little cycle ; 3. the element. For instance, the water-ox year of the fourteenth cycle is the year 1853. But in most cases the date is not given complete enough to be of much use. In the most ancient dates, as in the present case, only the animal's name is given. Some time between 1500 and 1600 the Ladakhis began to combine the animal's name with that of the element. Dates furnished also with the number of the cycle of sixty do not occur before the nineteenth century.

the Buddhist teacher *Atisa.* The best known of its kings are *Yeshes od* and *Jang chub od.*

On the accompanying map the empire of King Nyima gon with its three divisions is shown.

[*Drogon* and Chosgon, about 1025-1050, were the two sons of Lha chen palgyi gon.] As in several other cases, nothing besides the names is as yet known.

[*Lha chen dragspalde*, about 1050-1075, was the son of Drogon.]

[*Lha chen jang chub semspa*, about 1075-1100, was the son of the preceding.]

[*Lha chen rgyalpo*, about 1100-1125, the son of the preceding. He built the first real Lamasery in the country at *Likir* near Saspol, and caused a brotherhood of Lamas to settle down there.] *Likir* looks a little out of the way; but in those days *Likir* was a town on the great trade road. Before the present road along the Indus was cleared by the blasting of many rocks, the ordinary route to Leh was by Tingmogang, Hemis, and Likir. I have visited the monastery and found it a very stately building indeed; but its present shape seems to go back only to about the time when it adopted the reformed doctrine (see later). Still, its foundations and some of the wood-work and pictures are certainly old. Most of the wall-paintings were renovated recently. A very beautiful pencil-cedar close to the monastery is said to have been planted by Lha chen rgyalpo.

[Also the recluses that lived in the neighbourhood of the three lakes (Panggong, etc.) he provided for a long time, with untiring zeal, with the necessaries of life. When they were numerous there were about five hundred; when few, one hundred.]

In a popular saying, in which all the most ancient things of Ladakh are put together, the Likir monastery is given as the most ancient monastery, although those erected by Kashmiri monks are certainly older.

[*Lha chen Utpala*, about 1125-1150, the son of Lha chen rgyalpo. He united the forces of Upper and Lower Ladakh, subjected all the vassal chiefs, and even conquered a new province, Lowo, east of Purang]; so that his empire was perhaps even greater than that of Nyima gon. [All the vassal chiefs had to pay tribute and attend the annual council. He also invaded Kulu, and the King of Kulu bound himself by oath, "so long as the glaciers of the Kailasa do not melt away, or the Manasarowar Lake dry up, to pay his tribute to the King of Ladakh," in particular Dzos and iron.] This treaty remained in force at least down to the times of King Sengge namgyal. It may be asked: Why did he not annihilate the vassal princes? Eastern policy does not seem to have thought that advisable. Wars were only entered upon with the desire to fill one's pockets. These conquerors knew very well that a great deal more money could be squeezed out of a country if the old chieftain remained in it.

[*Lha chen Naglug*, about 1150-1175, the son of the former. This king built the palace at Wanla in the tiger year, and Kalatse in the dragon year.]

With regard to the building of Kalatse, the following may be added: Before the advent of the Central Tibetans, there used to be a Dard colony at Kalatse. These Dards had their stronghold in a castle about a mile above the present village, on the brook. The ruins of this castle, as well as of extensive fields and watercourses, can still be seen in the valley. The local Dard chieftains of Kalatse had their castle on the bank of the Indus, to guard a bridge. This bridge was built in opposition to the Babu khar bridge, three miles off, probably to draw the trade to their own territories. King Naglug is credited with having built the *Bragnag* castle on the rock towering above Kalatse, and in the popular saying of all the most ancient things, cited above, the Kalatse castle is called the first castle in the country, and popular tradition adds that it had to accommodate sixteen families. Besides, King Naglug seems to have constructed the first bridge across the Indus in the very same place where the present bridge is. The reason was certainly to draw the trade to his new bridge and thus secure the taxes. There still exists a stone inscription in close vicinity to the present bridge, which records the first construction of a bridge in this place and gives the dragon year (the date given in the chronicles as the date of the building of Kalatse) as the date of the construction of the bridge. But the proper name of the king is not given. The inscription simply speaks of "the great king." The edict ends up with a threat to all who might feel inclined to damage the new bridge. And this threat may have been necessary, because the Dard kings of Kalatse may not have wished to see it exclusively used. The threat runs as follows:—

Whoever thinks evil of it in his heart,
Let his heart rot!
Whoever stretches his hand towards it,
Let his hand be cut off!
Whoever harms it with his eye,
May his eye become blind!
Whoever does any harm to the bridge,
May that creature be born in hell!

[*Lha chen gebhe* and Gebum, about 1175-1200, were the sons of Lha chen naglug.]

[*Lha chen Joldor*, about 1200-1225, was probably the son of Gebhe.]

[*Trashis gon (b Krashis mgon)*, about 1225-1250, was the son of Joldor.]

[*Lhargyal*, about 1250-1275. He was the son of Trashis gon.] According to my theory, propounded elsewhere, the full name of this king was *Lha chen Kunga namgyal*. This name has been preserved to us on an ancient sculpture near the village of Daru. The principal sculpture represents a *Vajrapani* (Phyagrdor) as its central figure. Vajrapani seems to have been the favourite deity of this king; for [he ordered a treatise on the Vajra point (the *rGynd rdorje rtsemo*) to be copied in gold. Besides this, he ordered two other voluminous Lamaist works to be copied in gold on indigo-tinted paper]. This is the first record of the introduction of Lamaist literature into Western Tibet.

[*Lha chen jopal* (*dpal*), about 1275-1300, the son of the preceding. This king performed royal as well as clerical duties to such perfection that he reached Nirvana.] In a popular song the happy days under King Jopal are described: under this king people became so rich that they wore hats of gold, and their mouths never became empty of tea and beer. Masters and servants alike spent their days in frolic and merriment.

[*Lha chen ngorub* (*dngos grub*), about 1300-1325, Jopal's

son. During the reign of this king the usage of novices going to Central Tibet was first introduced.] This arrangement was not only the death-blow to the Bon-religion of Ladakh, which had probably lingered on down to that time; it meant also the end of the ancient forms of Indian Buddhism, which had had their principal seats in the grand monasteries erected by the Kashmir emigrants. Individuality was stamped out, and Lhasa became a literary centre. Apart from this the nation of Western Tibet, which had a very great gift for poetry, was prevented from developing a national literature. Without the authority of Lhasa nothing could attain to any popularity; so we find that national literature, with few exceptions, is not found in the country. But the high standard of West Tibetan folklore shows plainly what a high position the literary genius of the people would have taken had it been given free and fair play. In accordance with his plan of bringing Central Tibetan literature to a prominent position in his country [this king ordered the colossal Tibetan Encyclopaedia of Lamaism, called Kangyur (a library of 108 volumes) to be copied twice, and a book of secret spells to be copied many times. He also repaired the monasteries which had been built by his ancestors, probably those in particular which had been built by Lha chen gyalpo at Likir and on the lakes. Not content with that, he made costly offerings to Buddha of gold, silver, copper, coral beads, pearls, etc.]

[*Lha chen gyalbu rinchen,* about 1325-1350, the son of Lha chen ngorub.] That is all that we learn about him from the Ladakhi chronicles, and it is strange that no more is said of him, because for three generations before him the accounts have been a little fuller and grow in fulness after him. It is also remarkable that he is called *gyalbu,* prince. The epithet *lha chen,* great god, is the common title of all West Tibetan kings. An explanation is found in the chronicles of Kashmir, the famous Raja tarangini. Although the second part of this historical work, after 1150, by Jonaraja, has not yet been critically treated by a great scholar, we know enough of it to trace Prince Rinchen's career. The following is quoted from Sir Walter Lawrence's account of the history of Kashmir :—

"At the beginning of the fourteenth century, when Simha

Deva was king, Kashmir was a country of drunkards and gamblers. It was a most fitting time for the Tartar king Zulkadar Khan to invade the country. Helpless Simha Deva fled to Kishtawar, and the Tartars slaughtered the people, took slaves, and set fire to the city of Srinagar. After an occupation of eight months, the Tartars, who had depopulated the valley, found provisions scarce and tried to get out of Kashmir by the southern passes, but snow overtook them, and Zulkadar Khan and his army and his Kashmiri captives perished.

"Meanwhile Ram Chand, the commander-in-chief of Simha Deva, had been trying to keep up some semblance of authority in the valley, and when the Tartars departed he moved down and drove out the Gaddis, who had come in on a raid.

"Ram Chand had with him two men who were destined to play an important part in the history of Kashmir. One was Shah Mirza, from Swat, at whose birth it was prophesied that he would become king of Kashmir; the other was *Rainchan Shah*, who, having quarrelled with his father, the king of Tibet, came as an adventurer to the valley.

"Rainchan Shah (or Rinchana Bhoti, Rinchen the Tibetan, as he is called by Cunningham) seems to be none other than the Tibetan 'Prince Rinchen.' It has always been the custom among the West Tibetan kings to make the heir-apparent assistant to his father, when he reached manhood. As regent, Rinchen held different opinions from his father. Rinchen left Ladakh apparently after a son had been born to him, for there is no break in the line of succession.

"Before many days passed, Rainchan Shah broke with Ram Chand, and, with the assistance of his Tibetans, attacked and killed him. This took place at *Lahara kotta*, the present *Lar*, in the Sind valley. He then married *Kuta Rani*, Ram Chand's daughter, and proclaimed himself king, 1323 A.D. (Cunningham calls the daughter Ram Chand, and her father Sena Deva. He gives 1315, and, in another place, the middle of the fourteenth century as the date of the event. Also J.C. Dutta's date, 1323, is only approximately correct. Thus we may say that the event took place some time between 1315 and 1350.)

"Rainchan Shah, who had no strong convictions, found it necessary to adopt one or the other forms of faith which existed in Kashmir. He could not become a Hindu, because none of the Hindu castes would admit him to their brotherhood. One morning he saw a Mohammedan at his prayers, and, admiring this form of devotion, he adopted Mohammedanism and took the name of *Sadr ud din*. He built the Jama mosque and a great shrine for Bulbul Shah, the man whose devotion he had admired. The shrine is still known by the name 'Bulbul Lankar.'

"After a short reign of two and a half years Rinchen, the first of the Mussulman kings of Kashmir, died. His widow married first a brother of the old king, Simha Deva, and afterwards Shah Mirza, who became king of Kashmir and thus fulfilled the prophecy about him."

It is incredible that the news of Rinchen's accession to the throne of Kashmir was not made known in Ladakh. That no mention is made of this in the Tibetan chronicles may be due to his change of religion. That is the sin which the Lamas who wrote the chronicles could not forgive, and we shall meet with a very similar case later on.

It may be said that Rainchan Shah could just as well have hailed from Zangskar, Purig, or Baltistan. That is quite possible, but, in the absence of any historical records about these countries, we are glad that there are three distinct facts which point to the identity of Gyalbu Rinchen with Rainchan Shah, viz., 1. the coincidence of time; 2. the identity of the name; 3. the fact that the Tibetan record speaks of Rinchen only as a "prince."[1]

[*Lha chen shesrab*, about 1350-1375, the son of Gyalbu Rinchen. He built the hamlet *Sengge sgang* on the top of the *Hangtsemo* rock, at Sabu, six miles south-east of Leh, and made it a dependency of the *Chang* castle at Sabu.] The Chang castle was apparently one of the royal castles which, in the absence of the king, was occupied by his nominee, who received taxes from all the villages round about. I visited the site, and people told me that the rock was called Hlangtsemo (*glang rtsemo*) and the castle *Shangkar* or even Sangkar; but the name of the village *Sengge sgang* was not known. Local tradition

1. Another account of Prince Rinchen's career, according to material supplied by Dr Vogel, is given in the Appendix.

still speaks of the *Sangkar* castle as the beginning of Sabu. The site is on the ridge of mountains west of Sabu, and I found the hillside covered with ruined houses. It does not seem to have been occupied for a long time. The eastern side of the valley being more sunny, the king's minister moved there with the whole population, and built the village of Sabu and the "minister's castle," which is now in ruins. An ancient chorten below the ruined village of *Sengge sgang* seems to go back to the time of its creation. On one of the last hills at the end of the western range of mountains are the ruins of a watch-tower which enabled the ministers of Sabu to overlook the country from their castles.

[*Lha chen tri tsug lde* (*Khri btsug lde*), about 1375-1400, the son of Shesrab. He built one row of chortens numbering 108 at Leh, and two such rows at Sabu.] These rows of chortens, which were the forerunners of the mani-walls of which we shall hear later on, usually consist of chortens not higher than two or three feet, and in their dilapidated condition resemble low walls, built at random anyhow across the desert. But those built by kings are at least six feet high. Of those at Sabu there is still a fragment left, of about six yards. It looks as if the other portion of it had been carried away by a flood.

This is the last of the ancient kings, about whom we have but scanty information; and before we enter the next period of history, let us listen to a passage from the ancient epic on King Nyima gon.

Oh Father Nyima gon,
Do not go a-hunting !
In my dream last night
I saw something bad in my dream.
I, a boy, had to die !
I saw the colour of blood on my golden saddle.
I shall no more dance to the sound of trumpets and clarinets.
Oh king, do not go a-hunting,
Thy son Zlava gon has to die !

7

The Days of the Great Reformer Tsongkapa, and the Fall of the First Dynasty, about 1400-1580

FROM 1378-1441 A.D.[1] there lived in Tibet a great Lama, whose name was Tsongkapa. He found the Buddhism of Tibet in at least as rotten a state as it is now, and determined to reform it. He sat down to study the writings of the founder of this religion, and soon discovered that there were great discrepancies between what ought to have been and the actual facts. Among other discoveries which he made in the field of Lamaism was this, that the dress of the Lamas in no way corresponded with that of the early Buddhists. It was red and theirs yellow. Thus he resolved to found a new sect called the "virtuous ones," and to raise the moral standard of the monks to the standard, if possible, of the early Indian Buddhist monks. He would also have liked to exchange the red dress for the yellow, but public opinion seems to have been against it. People had got so much accustomed to the red garment of the Lamas that they would not have shown respect to a Lama in yellow dress. Thus Tsongkapa contented himself with the introduction of yellow caps and scarves. And, as with the dress, so it was with the morals. They could be raised only as high as public opinion would permit them to be.

About 1400 A.D. there were two kings in Western Tibet. Tri tsug lde had two sons: *Lha chen dragspa bum lde*, popularly called *Lde*, and *Dragspa bum*, generally known as *Dragspa*. Although Lde was the eldest and ought to have been king alone, Dragspa would not yield, and took possession of part

1. These numbers are given in Grunwedel and Pander's *Pantheon*. Sarat Chandra Das gives 1418 as the year of Tsongkapa's death.

of the kingdom. The two brothers were of very different character. Lde was of a mild and merciful disposition; Dragspa was fierce, gloomy, and inconsiderate. Lde was religiously inclined; Dragspa did not care in the least about his future state. Lde was thoughtful about even the low-caste people among his subjects; Dragspa could not bear the idea of having a brother king beside him.

[Lde commenced his career with the erection of a number of religious buildings. First he erected the "Red College," probably the one on the Namgyaltsemo hill behind Leh, and, perhaps on the same hill, a wood and clay statue of Maitreya, in a sitting posture, 25 feet high. There is a statue of this description on Namgyaltsemo hill, the head of which reaches through the ceiling of the first story. But the statues of Manjushri and Vajrapani, which are said to have been on the right and left, are no more, although there are traces of the pedestal of at least one of them. Many frescoes which this king is reported to have caused to be painted can be seen in the same temple. He also built a triple temple, one surmounting the other, on the pattern of an ancient temple erected by King *Yeshes od* of Zangskar at Toling, about 954, on the Upper Sutlej.] Where that is has not yet been traced.

With more certainty the sites of the following edifices can be fixed : [The little monastery, for four Lamas, which he built on the crag resembling an elephant, in the lower part of the Leh valley, the ruins of which are still extant; and the colossal chorten, the largest in all Ladakh, which he built over the "Yellow Crag," about one mile above Leh. It was erected because some "fatality" had occurred at Leh]. This sounds rather mysterious, but I think that the results of modern excavations, carried on occasionally by some of the missionaries, throw some light on the matter. We discovered in close vicinity to the chorten an ancient grave, with numerous entire skeletons, the skulls of which were of distinctly dolicho-cephalic shape, and several well-preserved clay-pots, some of which were ornamented with a dark red design. As far as we can make out, this grave goes back to Dard times. Another grave was discovered close by, but not opened. There seem to be a number of other graves in the neighbourhood. The "fatality" which had occurred at Leh was probably a serious illness of some important personage or an infectious disease, and the spirits of the old Dards who roamed about in the vicinity were suspected to be the authors. To make their excursions ineffective the magic power of a huge chorten seems to have been considered sufficient. Thus over the ancient burial-ground [the *Teu trashi od to* was erected, containing 108 temple shrines, and of the shape of a chorten]. When King Lde had done all this he believed he had gained enough religious merit, for he said : [If I die now it matters not].

But there was more in store for him to do; for about that time an embassy from the famous Tsongkapa arrived in Ladakh. Of this event the chronicles say : [At that time it came to pass that the Omniscient of the period of degeneration, the great Tsongkapa, having in his possession a Tse pag med (literally "eternal life") about as long as a finger-joint, which originated from the blood of his nose (I believe that it was a short summary of his doctrines, perhaps written with his own blood), entrusted the same to two ascetics and said : "Give it either to the one called Dragspa, or to the one called Lde!" When the two arrived in Western Tibet, the one called Dragspa was in Nubra. They went into his presence, but he did not deign to look at it with so much as one eye. So they went on to Leh. On the morrow the king gave command, "At today's council, whoever attends, be it ascetic or a low-caste man, Bheda,[1] Mon, or Shoemaker, he should not be refused admittance." Now, when the two ascetics came into his presence, the king rose and went to meet them. They made over the present, and the king was delighted with it].

The first consequence of the reformer's embassy was that King Lde [built the Spitug monastery; though in reality he did not build it, but it came into existence by a miracle]. This monastery was the first in Ladakh of "the virtuous sect," founded by Tsongkapa. The most important other monasteries of the same sect in Ladakh which were founded in course of time

1. Bheda is a Sanskrit word meaning "difference." As the caste of the Bhedas is still lower than that of the Mons. I believe that they are the descendants of the servants of the ancient Mons, who by their name had pointed out that they were not equal to them.

by other kings were : the Sangkar monastery near Leh, the Rirdzong monastery near Hemis shugpachan (this is not yet a century old), and the Trigtse monastery, twelve miles above Leh on the Indus. Several other monasteries exchanged the old doctrine for the new; for instance, Likir. [King Lde caused many brotherhoods of Lamas to settle in the country.]

From what has been said it would appear that King Lde's piety was no more than outward form. From an edict carved on the living rock at Mulbe we learn, however, that his religious sense was of a high type, and that it was his earnest desire to purify the Buddhism of his country. One of the best known doctrines of Buddhism is the prohibition to take animal life. But although Buddhism had been the religion of Western Tibet for many centuries, people had always shown a remarkable laxity with regard to the execution of this commandment. Not only were the people great hunters, but also the cruel sacrifices of living animals before the altars of pre-Buddhist deities were not yet abolished. At least once or twice a year a goat is offered before those altars in every village, when the heart is torn out of the living animal. The edict of Mulbe is directed against this cruel rite. It runs as follows :—

"Oh Lama (Tsongkapa), take notice of this! The king of faith, Bum lde, having seen the fruit of works in the future life, gives order to the men of Mulbe to abolish, above all, the living sacrifices, and greets the Lama. The living sacrifices are abolished."

It is not likely that Lde would have published his edict at Mulbe only, but in the other villages it was perhaps written on wooden boards. At any rate, in spite of special investigations, no other edict of a similar character has as yet been discovered.

But with the removal of sacrifices the king was no more successful than Tsongkapa with the reformation of the Church. Public opinion was against it, and we find the opinion of the people of Mulbe expressed in an inscription on the same rock, by the side of the edict in which they call King Lde's order too hard to be executed. For what would the local deity say, if the goat were withheld from him?

Meanwhile Dragspa had gone his own way. [His principal

seats were the villages of Basgo and Teya Tingmogang. He is called the builder of the royal city of Tingmogang] Here it is as it is with Kalatse. We must not imagine that there was nothing in the place before he came. From the Balu kar inscription it appears likely that there was a village called Tingbrang in the same valley in olden times; and a stone image, which is of striking similarity to those of Gilgit, would point to an originally Dard occupation of the place. But Dragspa built the now ruined town on the top of a low hill and its extensive fortifications, together with a stately castle above the town, and several watch-towers higher up. It was probably also Dragspa who improved the ancient fortifications at Basgo, to make them a stronghold of the first rank. In a great number of inscriptions after him, it is the castles at Basgo and Tingmogang, besides the palace erected later on at Leh, which are praised as the most valuable possessions of the Ladakhi kings. We heard that Dragspa was in Nubra at the time of Tsongkapa's embassy. What was he doing there ? we many ask; but no answer is given in the chronicles. I believe, however, that he went there to draw the local chief of Nubra over to his side, in order to make himself supreme king.

[*Lodros chog ldan* (*blo gros mchog ldan*), about 1440-1470. King Lde had three sons, the eldest of whom, Lodros chog ldan, became supreme king after him. It appears strange that the second of his sons had the half Mohammedan name Dungpa Ali. Could one of Lde's queens have been a Mohammedan lady?[1]

But also Dragspa had a son who became king after him in the villages which he had made his own.

Lodros chog ldan's reign began under good auspices. The chronicles say : [Having conquered Ngaris skor sum (Western

1. According to the Kashmir chronicles Sultan *Zainu-l-abidin's* expedition to Ladakh took place during the latter part of his reign, and perhaps *Bum lde* was compelled to marry a Mohammedan lady. Of this expedition the following is said : *Zainu-l-abidin*, King of Kashmir, invaded *Gogga-desha* (probably Guge) and saved a golden image of Buddha from the hands of the Mohammedans (his own soldiers ?) in *Shaya-desha* (probably the village of Sheh). Then he took the town of Kuluta (*Kula*) (Kulu).

Tibet), his dominions grew much in extent]. This can only mean that all the vassal chiefs were subdued once more, and that the King of Leh was the real master of the empire. His greatest triumph was [the arrival of vast quantities of presents and tribute from Guge in the east; fifty grey ponies, fifty isabel, twenty black, and thirty piebald ones; twenty young yak-cows, and twenty light-brown (a very rare colour) yak-bulls; sheep in immense quantities, and very valuable weapons. All these weapons had appropriate names, and the most striking among them were "the resplendent devil-coat-of-mail," the coat-of-mail "devil darkness," the white "gods" coat-of-mail; the sword "licking blood off the sky," the sword "wild yak, long point," the sword "killer of the red lightning flame"; the "black devil knife." Besides these, fifteen turquoises of great value were brought, and twenty saddles].

Lodros chog ldan's reign seems to have lasted long; for when the blow against the dynasty was struck it did not come from Dragspa's son, Bhara, but from his grandson, Bhagan.

[*Lha chen Bhagan*, about 1470-1500. He and the people of Sheh (a village eight miles south-south-east of Leh, on the Indus), having formed an alliance, deposed and subjected the sons of the King of Leh, Lodros chog ldan, and his two brothers.] Thus the kingdom of Lodros chog ldan, which had nothing to fear from external enemies, became an easy prey to its internal foes, as soon as they managed to bring the greater weight of power on their side. What was the lot of the last members of the old dynasty is not stated. Bhagan is the founder of the second, or Namgyal, dynasty, which lasted down to the end of the empire. He called his two sons Namgyal, or "perfect victors," and the word Namgyal combined with other names, is found in the names of all his descendants.[1] [This

1. It seems to have been a general custom in Tibet to use certain names as dynastical names. Thus the word *tsan* or *tsanpo*, is found in a great number of names of the ancient Central Tibetan dynasty, and the words Lha chen, great god, were combined with most names of the first Western Tibetan dynasty. As, however, the second dynasty descended from the first, the name of Lha chen was added, at pleasure, to the names of many of its members.

king was very fond of fighting) is said of Bhagan; but we do not hear of any more of his wars.

[*Lhawang namgyal* (*Lha dbang rnam rgyal*) and *Trashi* (*bKrashis*) *namgyal*, about 1500-1530. The bad example set by their father showed its influence on the sons. Once more the younger brother's ambition strove after the crown. The brothers are characterised as follows: Lhawang had great bodily strength and was clever at any kind of sport; but Trashi was very crafty. To attain his aim, Trashi caused his elder brother's eyes to be plucked out. Then he sent him to Lingshed on the borders of Zangskar.] But then a strange circumstance which the Ladakhis regard as the judgment of heaven occurred: Trashi remained without children and there was great danger [that the dynasty would die out. Therefore Trashi gave his blind brother a wife]. From a votive tablet at Tingmogang we learn that Lhawang outlived Trashi, and that there was some glory about his old days. For after Trashi had died, the new king, Lhawang's son, took his father back to the capital (Tingmogang in those days), and blind Lhawang received full honours as "father-king."

[The first thing the crafty Trashi had to do was to conquer once more the whole country and subdue the vassal-chiefs. As he also conquered Droshod, he prepared the way for the conquests of the next king, under whom the Western Tibetan kingdom reached its greatest extension. His principal spoils were ponies, of which he brought great quantities to Ladakh. He then built the first royal palace at Leh, on the top of the Namgyaltsemo hill, and below it the hamlet of Chubi.] The greater part of this palace is now in ruins, but some of its ancient walls were used when the present monastery on the top of that hill was built. Also some of the watch-towers which were built in connection with the palace still remain. [He also erected a temple dedicated to the lords of the four quarters on the same hill, and thus obtained power over the demon that turns back hostile armies. That power he had acquired in the nick of time, for just then an army of Turks invaded the country. He fought against them and killed many; and, apparently, as a thank-offering, the corpses of the Turks were placed under the images of the lords of the four quarters.]

After that Trashi thought it advisable to turn his thoughts towards religion; for he was, not without reason, afraid that his stock of accumulated merit might be rather small. But his religion was not of the reformed class; the craftier, the better. Therefore, [according to the advice of the great Lama Ldanma of Drikhung in Tibet, he built a monastery of the red sect at Piang, which is one of the most imposing building in the country. At the spot where this Lamasery is seen for the first time (probably coming from Leh), he placed a long prayer-flag. Whosoever, whether thief or liar, in short anyone guilty of offence against the king's palace or life, if he escaped to this spot, should be rid of his crime.

He made the rule regarding the number of children that were to be sent by every village to become Lamas]. According to it, every family of more than one or two male children had to give up one, not the eldest, however, to be made a Lama. Now that this rule is no longer compulsory, there has been a great falling off in the number of Lamas.

(Finally, Trashi made the usual offerings of goldwater (for writing books with gold characters), prayer flags, cushions, tea, etc., to the most famous Central Tibetan monasteries, and caused a number of religious books, among them the Encyclopaedia, to be copied. He even erected many chortens], but it is not stated which they are.

(*Tsewang namgyal I.* (*Thse dbang*), about 1530-1560. Blind King Lhawang had three sons: Tsewang namgyal, Namgyal gonpo, and Jamyang namgyal. They all grew very tall in stature; they grew taller in a month than others grow in a year; and they grew taller in a day than others grow in a month.) This passage sounds exactly as if it had been taken from the Kesar saga.

Tsewang ascended the throne without having to be afraid of a pretender. It was as if the time of the civil wars was now coming to an end. [When quite a young man, Tsewang had to go to war, because the vassal-chiefs believed they had got another chance of making themselves free. However, they were all subdued, and under him the Western Tibetan empire reached its greatest extension. In the south the chiefs of Kulu were made to feel the weight of his arm:[1] he even conquered a portion of Baltistan. To end the continual warfare against the vassal-chiefs, he brought the rulers of all the conquered districts with him as hostages, and placed his own representatives in their castles. He also said he would make war against the Turks, north of Ladakh; but the people of the frontier province Nubra, who were afraid of harm being done to the trade to Yarkand, petitioned him to abstain from that war, and he desisted.

The tribute which came to Ladakh in his days was very great. Again we are told what was received from Guge: 900 grammes of gold annually. From Rutog came 780 grammes of gold annually, and in addition 100 three years' sheep, one riding-horse, ten tanned skin-bags, and the proceeds from the royal domains near Rutog.)

Tsewang seems to have been a really ingenious man. To carry on his campaigns, roads and bridges were needed, and two records of road-building under him have been discovered, one on the road to Baltistan, near the Hanu gorge, the other on the way to Zangskar, at Hunupata. Tsewang wished to keep the goodwill of the people, which he was in danger of losing if he charged them with the construction of the bridge at Hunupata as part of the ordinary forced labour system. He therefore proclaimed that the building of the bridge was a means for everybody to accumulate religious merit, and that the names of all those who had some share in the work would be embodied in the inscription. Through this arrangement he made certain of the goodwill of the people, and at the same time got the bridge. The minister who superintended the work was Bumbha lde, and in a popular song we are told he made liberal use of the cane. In the song old Bumbha is teased by the people, who are no more afraid of him. Tsewang belongs to the popular kings whose names are not yet forgotten. His nephew Sengge namgyal built the Alchi bridge several years later, according to the same system.

To do also something in the cause of religion [Tsewang

1. The conquest of Kulu included that of Lahoul, which is mentioned in the chronicles of Lahoul.

planned the erection of a college on the Namgyaltsemo hill, because his ancestors had not succeeded in making this hill a place of pilgrimage, although they had placed the bones of Buddha in his elephant incarnation on the top of the hill. But, as his work on earth was finished, he died].

This chapter has shown us that, in spite of old and reformed Buddhism, most of the Western Tibetan kings had their minds directed to the things of this world. That also other people were not much different is shown by *Ladakhi Songs*, No. VI.

The high ones live in high places.
Into all the heights of the sky,
Besides the king of birds, none flies.
During the three summer months
Whatever can bloom, blooms.
Except in the three summer months,
Oh, there are no flowers.
Besides this one lifetime
I shall not belong to my mother,
In this one lifetime
Whatever can be happy, is happy.
Enjoy this one lifetime
As ever you can enjoy it.

8

The Time of the Balti Wars, about 1560-1640

THE population of Baltistan, as well as that of the rest of Western Tibet, consists of Aryan and Tibetan elements; but, as has been supposed by several writers, in Baltistan the Dard element is somewhat stronger than in other parts of the country, and this may account for certain superiorities in the character of the Baltis. The Balti is, as history proves, rather braver than the average Western Tibetan; he is quicker in adopting new methods and altogether more alert.

The last we had heard of the Baltis was their brave resistance against the Chinese conquerors, in the eighth century. The tenth century brought the conquest of practically the whole of Western Tibet by *Nyima gon*, and it is at least probable that in those wars Baltistan was also concerned, although nothing is said in the Tibetan chronicles. As we know from ancient inscriptions and sculptures, the religion of the Baltis was a Tibetan form of Buddhism, and the Tibetan alphabet was at least partly known. Besides this, the Baltis pride themselves also on having an ancient alphabet running from right to left.

The Baltis apparently never had a king over themselves who was the undisputed master of the whole country; they had *magspons* or dukes instead, who took a leading part only in time of war. But for periods a certain famous magspon seems to have had the command over the united forces of all Baltistan.

The Baltis were the first Western Tibetans who became Mussulmans. Although we have no definite record to go by, Cunningham makes it probable that the change of religion took place some time about 1400. His method is the following:

Cunningham collected the pedigrees of six magspon families of Baltistan and compared them with each other. None of them is of very great historical value, as the magspons, on their becoming Mohammedans, ignored their origin from Tibetan or Dard Buddhist ancestors, and fabricated new pedigrees with as many Mussulman names in them as possible. The most important and probably most ancient magspon family was that of Kapulu, and its fabricated pedigree of sixty-seven members (in 1830) starts with a Sultan Sikander, after whom the Sultans Ibrahim and Ishak are placed. The fact that Sikander is placed at the head of this pedigree makes Cunningham suspect that the introduction of Mohammedanism into Baltistan may have taken place about the time of Sikander, the Iconoclast, who reigned in Kashmir about 1380-1400.

Jamyang namgyal, about 1560-1590. Tsewang had died unexpectedly, without leaving any children, and therefore one of his younger brothers had to take up the reins of government. Why *Namgyal gonpo*, who was the next, did not become king, is not stated. We are simply told that Jamyang reigned. Unfortunately, all the vassal-kings whom Tsewang had carefully brought to Leh had found an opportunity to escape, and [they all lifted up their heads]. Thus the first task Jamyang had to master was to fight them all, one after another.

He turned his attention first of all to Purig. In this country great changes were taking place, as the two chiefs of that country, the Princes of Chigtan and Kartse, had adopted Mohammedanism and styled themselves Sultans. According to Chigtan traditions, Tsering malik, who then reigned, was the first Mohammedan chief of that part of Purig. It is quite possible that these two princes embraced Mohammedanism only to alienate their subjects from the rest of the Ladakhis, whose suzerainty had always been unpleasant to them. Fortunately for Jamyang, the two new Sultans quarrelled with one another, and Jamyang decided to go to the assistance of Tsering malik of Chigtan.

Popular tradition has the following about the beginning of this campaign : "It was late in the year when the Ladakhi army was on the point of starting, and it was not considered lucky to start before having celebrated the New Year's festival.

However, to wait for the Tibetan New Year would have meant a delay of two months. Therefore Jamyang, who was not particularly energetic in other respects, had energy enough to decide that this year the New Year's festival was to be celebrated two months before it actually fell. Ever since, New Year has been celebrated about two months earlier in Ladakh than in Central Tibet."

In spite of these measures to hasten his campaign, Jamyang started on it too late. The whole business looks rather like a trap into which he was enticed. For the Baltis, who had not yet forgotten Tsewang's inroads, were only waiting for an opportunity to pay off this old debt. [Ali Mir, the Duke of Kapulu, had united under his sway the forces of all Baltistan, and as soon as the Ladakh army had crossed the passes towards Purig the Balti forces broke forth. The armies met; but by dint of stratagem, ever putting off fighting from one day to the next, Ali Mir succeeded in holding the Ladakhis on, until all the passes and valleys were blocked with snow, and the king with his army, wherever they went, were compelled to surrender.] But the snow apparently formed no obstacle to the Baltis, for [all Ladakh was soon overrun by the Baltis, who burnt all the religious books with fire, threw others into the water, and destroyed all the colleges; whereupon they returned to their own country]. In short, they behaved like true Mohammedans and iconoclasts. They had some time before cleared their own country of idols and Buddhist remains, and were now enjoying the same sport in Ladakh.

Truly it may be said of Ladakh that [the time had now come when the period of darkness should supervene, the period when royal supremacy should well-nigh be destroyed]; and the proverb "At the tricks of the plucky Balti the heart of the timid Ladakhi is lost," was probably coined in those days.

Practically, the Western Tibetan kingdom had come to an end. The king was Ali Mir's prisoner, and the army was annihilated. Just then [it pleased Ali Mir Sher Khan, as his full name was, to give his daughter, *Gyal Katun* by name, to Jamyang namgyal, to be his wife]. Although the lady was certainly very beautiful, the marriage had its taste of bitterness, for Jamyang was obliged to make Gyal Katun his first wife, and to disinherit the sons who had been born by his old queen. Still, the Lamas knew how to make matters more pleasant. They found out that (Katun was an incarnation of the White Tara). Who would not give up any woman for that distinguished lady ? It was rather startling that the White Tara should have chosen the body of a Mohammedan girl for an incarnation; but women are capricious, and the White Tara is quite capable of being re-born sometime as a Papuan lady.

Ali Mir's principal object in marrying Jamyang to his daughter was, as I suppose, to draw him quietly over to Mohammedanism, and it is surprising that this did not happen after all.

On a rock at Mulbe is carved a wedding congratulation to Jamyang and his new queen. Soon after the wedding Ali Mir had a remarkable dream which proved to be of the greatest importance to his son-in-law. [Now, after Ali Mir had prepared a feast for all the soldiers, and Gyal Katun had put on all her jewels, he invited Jamyang namgyal to mount the throne, and then said : "Yesterday I dreamt I saw a lion emerging from the river in front of the palace and jumping at Gyal Katun; he disappeared into her body. At the very same time also Gyal Katun conceived. Now it is certain she will give birth to a male child, whose name ye shall call Sengge namgyal (lion, conqueror of all)." Having said this, he gave the king leave to return home with the army of Ladakh, and to resume his royal functions.]

Thus the Ladakhi empire was saved, but its size was now smaller than it had ever been, and as after his sad experiences the king did not feel inclined to fight once more against the vassal princes, he called his own only the country from Purig (Purig apparently not included) to Drangtse, near the Panggong Lake.

Although his misfortune was due to the strategic superiority of a Mussulman king, Jamyang decided to do all in his power to strengthen the much shaken Buddhism of Ladakh. [He said: "I will employ any means that may serve towards the propagation of the religion of Buddha and make it spread. But, as the religion of Buddha for its propagation is entirely dependent on the people, I will, on my part, relieve them from taxation and treat them like my own children." Having thus resolved, he equalised rich and poor three times.] It is a pity we are not told how the rich liked this proceeding.

Purig, however, could not be regained for Buddhism, for the two new Sultans made use of their independence, and Mohammedanism became their state religion. Still, in the territory of the Purig Sultans of Chigtan, the progress of Mohammedanism was remarkably slow, and even nowadays a traveller to this district can make interesting observations with regard to the half-Lamaist kind of Mohammedanism prevailing there. The old Onpos, or astrologers, find it still easy to make a living, and the once famous monastery of Chigtan is visited annually by large crowds who deposit their flower-offerings, as had been the custom in Buddhist times. On account of this attachment of the people to the monastery, the monks did not desert it at once, and the last Buddhist monk, called Gergan (*dGe rgan*) Tsering, left the place about 1860. I have met people who had seen him. This old monastery, as well as the imposing castle of the chiefs of Chigtan, are well worth a visit. The people of Tağmachig, who were subject to these chiefs, did not like the change of religion, and, as their now lost inscription is said to have told, they went to the Ladakhi king, Jamyang's successor, and asked him to allow them to become his subjects. They were accepted, and remained Buddhists.

To set an example to his subjects, Jamyang sent a deputation with costly presents to the principal Central Tibetan monasteries, and the sons who were born by his old, now deposed, queen, had to escort them and later on to act as messengers to a high Lama. This was a convenient way to get rid of them. One of them, *Ngag wang namgyal*, became the principal Lama of Lahoul.

[After he had ordered a number of Lamaist books to be copied in gold, silver, and copper, he would have much liked to rebuild and present anew whatsoever had been destroyed by the Baltis; but, his life being short, he died before he had been able to accomplish his purpose.] The best known ruins of the Balti wars are : the Nyizlapug monastery at Saspola; the Kaoche monastery at Spitug; and the Lingshed castle and monastery.[1]

Sengge namgyal, about 1590-1620. He was the son of Jamyang and Katun, and had inherited the warlike spirit of his grandfather, Ali Mir. [From his childhood he was very strong and clever at wrestling, running, jumping, shooting with bow and arrow as well as matchlock, and riding.

In any kind of sport he was to be compared with Prince Siddharta Gautama of olden times.

He was married to a Rubshu princess, called Skal Zang], and this is one of the few queens who have acquired some real fame. On almost all of the many inscriptions of the time of this king we find the queen mentioned and praised, and also their children were apparently general favourites.

In spite of his Mohammedan mother, this king does not appear to have had any liking for Mohammedanism, and Buddhism was strengthened in the crown provinces more than had been the case for some time. This was in particular the work of the great Lama [Stag tsang ras chen, whom Sengge namgyal had invited to Ladakh. This great Buddha had visited Hindustan, Urgyan (Udyana), and Kashmir, and had seen all the eighty saints face to face].

This great Lama, whose name is still in the people's mouth, is said to be the author of the well-known book of travel called *The Journey to Shambhala*, and he is either the inventor of the mani-walls or the introducer of them to Ladakh. For some time I made the mani-walls my special field of research, and have read the votive tablets of a great number of them, but have not found a single wall that was erected before the time of Sengge namgyal. There is a special kind of them, "two storied" type, which dates almost exclusively from the time of this king.

1 According to Cunningham, during the attempts to restrengthen Buddhism in Ladakh, the colossal stone Maitreya at Mulbe is said to have been probably erected. This is quite improbable, as such an event would certainly be mentioned in the chronicles. Besides, the custom of erecting stone images is very much older. Judging from the few dateable ones, we may say that not many were erected after 1000 A.D. The Mulbe image was probably carved by one of the Purig chiefs during their first time of independence.

The "two-storied" kind has a narrower upper storey than the lower one, and therefore somewhat resembles a damaged row of 108 chortens, as were built in earlier times. In fact, several rows of chortens seem to have been turned into the two-storied type of mani-wall. There is one of this kind at Kalatse. But the one-storied, and more common, type of mani-wall came up already under this king. Such a wall with an inscription, mentioning Sengge namgyal, I have discoverd at Lingshed, and the large mani-walls outside Basgo are said by popular tradition to have been erected by Stag tsang ras chen.

Stag means tiger, and *sengge*, lion, and the fame of the "tiger-Lama" and the "lion-king" are still remembered, and the chronicles have the following passage on the two : [The king governed over all his dominions according to the ten virtues, and thus it came to pass concerning the kingdom of this world that the king was like the lion, and the Lama like the tiger, and their united fame encompassed the face of the earth as "the lord and the Lama," "sun and moon," a pair].

Sengge namgyal twice went to war, both times to the east. Purig and Baltistan he left undisturbed. Still, as we find from an inscription by him at Karbu, during his reign this part of Purig seems to have been considered his own. His son had to re-conquer it. The people of Tagma-chig assert that their lost inscription spoke of an expedition of Sengge namgyal against Baltistan. But they are probably mistaken.[1] [When yet a youth, he made war against the back steppes of Guge to re-conquer that lost province for his kingdom, and carried away ponies, yaks, goats, and sheep, even so far as from the northern slopes of Kailasa, and indeed from everywhere on earth. He made all Ladakh to be full of yaks and sheep. Some time later he made war against the central provinces of Guge also.

When he was old, he bethought himself : "My uncle Tse-wang namgyal certainly did rule over all the country as far as

1. Cunningham says that Sengge namgyal beat the Baltis with great slaughter at Karbu. But, as he also erroneously places the battle of Basgo (see below) under Deldan, instead of Delegs, it is very probable that also in this case he mixes up Sengge's reign with that of his son Deldan.

Ngamring in the east; but he did not live long, and during the reign of my father all the vassal-princes again rose and made themselves independent." So he again went to war, and came as far as Ngamring (only seven marches from Shigartse); but at Shirikarmo his army was routed. This place is situated on the right bank of the *Charta* River; and, as K. Marx observes, the difficulty of crossing the river may to some extent account for the defeat of the Ladakhi army. Upon this, there arrived an ambassador from Tibet, and it was agreed that the frontier should remain as before, and that Sengge namgyal's dominion should include all the country up to Ustsang, up to about the Charta River. On his return journey the king died at Hanle.]

Before this campaign Sengge namgyal had entered, in co-operation with the Lama, on a great scheme of grand building enterprises, many of which were finished long after his time by his son. The best known of these buildings is the Leh castle, above the city, a huge building of the nine stories which was completed in about three years. Another remarkable building is the Maitreya monastery at Basgo, above the ruins of the ancient fort. It still contains the statue of Maitreya of clay, copper and gilt, as big as he would be in his eightieth year, *i.e.* three stories high. More the work of the "tiger-Lama" than of the king are the four great Lamaseries which were erected at Hemis, Chemre, Trashisgany (nowadays in Tibet proper, beyond the frontier), and Hanle. Especially the Hemis monastery has become famous on account of the devil-dances which take place there every year in summer. Also a wooden bridge across the Indus was constructed under Sengge namgyal, at Alchi, according to an inscription.

[That King Sengge did not forget to have the Encyclopaedia and many other books copied in copper, silver, and gold; and that costly offerings of silk, gold, silver, corals, pearls, amber, etc., were sent to the Central Tibetan monasteries for the spiritual welfare of his father and Mussulman mother, can well be imagined. But the best bargain was made by "the tiger-Lama," who received 100 ponies, 100 yaks, 1000 sheep, 1000 rupees, 300 grammes of gold, 3000 loads of grain, 1 string of pearls, 1 string of coral beads, 1 string of turquoise beads, 25 match-locks, 25 spears, 25 swords, 15 coats-of-mail, 25 pieces of silk, 10 pieces of brocade, 25 pieces of gauze, 25 pieces of broad gauze for scarfs of blessing, and other presents.]

The form of religion of this king and his great Lama was that of the red sect, and all the monasteries built by them belong to Lamas of that persuasion. This form of religion has always shown a resemblance to Sivaism, and from that the words [he introduced the great deities of all Hindustan] become intelligible. Another not quite clear passage seems to mean that people were specially allowed to kill game, which would also imply a lax form of Buddhism.

Deldan namgyal, about 1620-1640, who became king after his father, was the eldest of Sengge namgyal's sons. His two brothers became vassal-kings under him. [Indra Bodhi namgyal, who had entered the clerical career as one of Stagtsang raschen's principal disciples, and acted as superintendent at the erection of the Hemis and Chemre Lamaseries, became ruler of Guge; and Dechog namgyal, the youngest, was made vassal-king of Zangskar and Spiti.] From this it appears that the ancient line of the Zangskar kings had come to an end.

When Deldan ascended the throne, his kingdom reached only from Purig to the Maryum Pass, but it was his ambition to restore the lost prestige of the Ladakhi army and to bring the rulers of Purig once more under his rule, besides avenging his family on the Baltis. These plans were not executed until he had reached old age, but they were eventually, and the Ladakhi kingdom attained to about the same fame and power under him as it had during its best times. As the many inscriptions prove, Deldan was also a very popular king, and if what we know about the lost inscription at Kalatse is true, he was not only a wise organiser, but also a ruler who took an interest in the welfare of his subjects. The inscription tells of his regulating the irrigation water in that village.

[Deldan did not show the same building activity as his father. He built only an Assembly Hall at Leh and the longest mani-wall in the country. It is the one at the Tewa Gorge, and is about 850 paces long. At the upper end there is a high chorten of the Namgyal type (with round steps), and at the lower end a high chorten of the Jangchub type (with square steps). This was built for the spiritual welfare of his mother;

and for that of his father he erected at Sheh an image of Buddha, of clay, copper and gilt, three stories high. Also a chorten, five stories high, was reared there. Another image of Buddha, two stories high, was constructed at the Leh palace, and one of Avalokitesvara, of the same height, probably at the Assembly Hall, where is also the silver chorten made by him, which is of the same height. I believe that most of Deldan's structures are still in existence. At each of the principal monasteries were placed 108 Lamas, who had to perform the one hundred millions of *Om mani padme hum* incantations once a year.

Then he appointed his minister, Shakya gyatso, Field-Marshal. In the water-ox year the Ladakh army took the field, and marched to Purig to re-conquer this lost province. The first territory they invaded was that of the Tri Sultan of Kartse, who was then independent king over the country from Karbu to Dras. Many men and women of Karbu they carried away captive, and the castles of Henasku and Stagtse were reduced and brought into subjection. Although the Tri Sultan had not yet been attacked in his capital, the army now invaded the territory of the other ruler of Purig, the Purig Sultan of Chigtan, and his strongest castles, Chigtan and Shagkar, were taken. When there was nothing more to fear from that side, the Ladakh Field-Marshal marched against the three strongest castles of the Tri Sultan. The first was Sod, a little north of Kargil, and after it had been taken the harvest of the fields in the vicinity was gathered in. The other two castles, Sumtang and Kartse, were then attacked and taken, and the Tri Sultan himself became a prisoner. He was transported to Leh.

In the wood-tiger year the Ladakh army marched against Baltistan, and conquered the villages Chorbar and Tortsekar. Over these districts were placed chieftains of the Ladakhis' choosing. The Duke of Skardo and all the Baltis were unanimous in their complaints to the Nawab (probably of Kashmir) of these high-handed proceedings. The Nawab induced the Turks to invade Ladakh, and an army of Turks, numbering 200,000 (probably 20,000) arrived at Pasari. But the minister Drug namgyal of Ladakh fought a battle against them and killed many Turks. They took away their flags and kettledrums, and thus gained a complete victory over the enemy.]

During the days of Deldan the mission of the Jesuit Andrada to Tsaparang in Guge seems to have taken place.

These glorious wars brought the Western Tibetan empire once more to the respected position it had once occupied. There are many popular songs which tell of wars against the Baltis, but it is very difficult to assign to them their proper place in history. Here are two specimens of them. The first *may* go back to the Buddhist times of Baltistan.

At the Lake Mondur, Stobsyabgopa appears and shows his strategy.
The god-like force of Skardo cast their lhassos of steel.
They pay back to the god-like army of Ladakh what is their due.
They revenge their fathers and forefathers on them.
The children of the Lord of Shigar gain a glorious victory.

The lord resides at the flower-castle of Saling.
God is gracious to thee this summer!
The king resides at the flower-castle of Saling.
God is giving success to thee this summer!
Thou turnest back the Turk army of Skardo on the Daltong Pass.
God is gracious to thee this summer!
Thou dictatest a treaty to them, to last longer than a lifetime.
Lightning flashes out of King Deldan namgyal's sword.[1]

1. The original has Deskyong namgyal, which is a mistake, as Deskyong did not carry on any wars.

9

The Great Mongol War, about 1646-1647

DURING the time from 1643-1716 A.D., Central Tibet was a dependency of Mongolia. The reason why the Mongolians had become masters of the country was the severe quarrels between the yellow-cap Lamas and the red-cap Lamas. A detailed account of these quarrels does not belong to the domain of Western Tibetan history, because in this country the two sects have always lived in peace with each other. Whoever is interested in these fights for supremacy may look them up in a Central Tibetan history. Now it was the red-cap sect, and soon after the yellow-cap sect, who asked the Mongolians to come to their support, and the result of the long wars was that the Mongol Gushri Khan seized the whole country and became king of united Mongolia and Tibet. He had fought for the cause of the yellow church, and made that church supreme in all his dominions.

It would have been very natural, if the thought had arisen in the minds of these great Mongol-Tibetan rulers, to add also the Western Tibetan empire to their dominions, and thus to become masters of the whole Lamaist world. But the thought does not appear to have occurred to them before war was declared from the Ladakhi side. The chronicles give the following reason for the beginning of hostilities.

[At the time of *Delegs namgyal*, about 1640-1680, Deldan's son, the Bhutan state had a quarrel with the Tibeto-Mongolian monarchy. Now, as the Pope of Bhutan was the patron Lama of the King of Ladakh, the latter sent a letter to Tibet, saying that he was prepared to take up his quarrel. The Tibetans, when hearing of this, instead of entering into any negotiations, raised an army at once, to prevent the Ladakhis from overrunning their country.

Magic calculations pointed to a Mongol Lama called Tsang, who was at the time residing at Galdan, as the destined leader. He, accordingly, turned layman, and, heading the Mongol tribe and a powerful army of Tibetans, soon reached Ladakh. At the beginning of active warfare it came to an engagement at Zhamarting, near the Panggong lake. The Ladakhis were driven back, and in time the Mongol army arrived at Basgo.]

One of the great mistakes of Delegs was that he did not go to war himself, but contented himself with sending his general. He may have thought that in this he was following the example of his father, but it looks rather as if he had been afraid of the battle-field. Now he did not even remain at splendidly fortified Basgo, where the greater portion of the Ladakhi army found shelter, but fled to the fortress of Tingmogang, about thirty miles further west. The fortress of Basgo seems to have had one great advantage, in a continual water-supply. None of the Western Tibetan fastnesses was in danger of running short of grain; for all these castles had tremendous storehouses of grain, which look like very deep, round masonry wells. They were not only filled when the enemy was before the doors; but it was a custom to throw some of the harvest into these pits every year, and thus the grain was ready at hand when the enemy arrived. In the storehouse at Wanla there is still some of this old grain left. Because the castles were so well provided, [the Ladakhi army held its own for three years.[1] But they were unable to drive the Mongol army back again]. And, as popular tradition knows, the Mongols went on raiding expeditions all over the country.

When the difficulties of Delegs had reached their highest point, [he dispatched a messenger to the Nawab of Kashmir], to come to his assistance. In those days Kashmir was a province of the great Mogul empire of India, and as the Nawab was one of the Mogul's officers, he sent Delegs' letter on to Delhi. In this manner the history of Ladakh

1. Six months, according to other historians

became connected with Mogul history, which has the great advantage that, with regard to this war, we have the privilege of consulting Mogul historians, in particular Mir Izzet Ullah (1812), cited by Cunningham and Bernier, the friend of Aurangzib, who has preserved the date of the battle of Basgo. At this time the bigoted Shah Jahan sat on the throne of the Moguls, and it looks very much like him to promise his assistance only on one chief condition, viz. that the Ladakhi king was to become a Mussulman in acknowledgement of it. There were several conditions of minor importance besides, which will be mentiond below. As Delegs was in a mood to promise anything, an army of 600,000 warriors, as the Mogul historians say, was dispatched under Nawab Fateh Khan and five other officers. The number of 600,000 is quite an impossibility. Never could such a host be fed in a barren country like Ladakh Cunningham proposes to say 6000 instead.

This army crossed the Indus at Kalatse on one rope and two wooden bridges, and advanced to Basgo. The Mongol army left the fortress and arranged itself in battle-order on the Jargyal plain between Basgo and Nyemo. [There a battle ensued. The Mongol army was routed; they left behind them a large quantity of armour, bows and arrows, and their rout continued until they reached Spitug. Even there they did not make a long halt, but continued their flight until they came to Trashisgang, beyond the Panggong lake. Unfortunately for Delegs, they did not flee any farther. But at Trashisgang they built a fort, shut it in with a wall, and surrounded it with water.]

After the Mogul army had rendered this great service to Delegs, he left Tingmogang and went to meet the Nawab, to express his very sincere thanks. But, alas, this was not considered sufficient, and the Nawab presented a bill to Delegs, which contained the following items:—

1. Delegs was to become a Mussulman and to accept the new name Akabal (or Akabat?) Mahmud Khan. This was not so very easy, considering the great power Buddhism had acquired in Ladakh under his father and grandfather, and the vengeance of the Lamas was certain to be cruel. As the news about Delegs' change of religion is very contradictory, I will

simply state what we hear about it.

The Mussulman historians speak of it quite in the affirmative, and therefore Cunningham is of opinion that the least we can accept is that Delegs was taken to the Nawab's camp, where he had to repeat the words of the Mohammedan creed as they were dictated to him. The Tibetan historians and the Lamas pretend to know nothing of a Mohammedan confession, and strictly deny such an occurrence.

Still, I believe that the Mogul historians are right, and the Lamas even betray themselves. As we have seen in the case of Rinchen Bhoti, it is the Lamas' policy to ignore, if possible, even the name of a king who was unfaithful to Buddhism. This they seem to have tried in the case of Delegs, as a study of the votive inscriptions of Ladakh reveals. Votive inscriptions of ordinary people, in which, besides the name of the sacrificer, the king's name, with patriotic good wishes, is given, are very frequent with reference to Deldan namgyal, Delegs' father, and Nyima namgyal, Deleg's son. But up to the present, I have not found a single votive tablet in which mention was made of "King" Delegs. The name Delegs namgyal occurs only on some of Deldan's tablets, where he is mentioned as Deldan's son. That there are no tablets in existence referring to Delegs' government, makes me believe that the Lamas either destroyed them all or forbade the people to mention this king on their tablets.

A very similar case is the following: The Ladakh chronicles speak of five sons of King Delegs, but give the names of only four of them. The name of the fifth, Jigpal namgyal, was crossed out, because he had to be sacrificed to Mohammedanism for the benefit of the whole country.

2. To make certain of Delegs' change of religion, [his wife and his son Jigpal—aJigs dpal—(the chronicles speak of "children"; perhaps some daughters were included) had to go to Kashmir, to stay there as hostages for three years]. As far as we know, they never came back to Ladakh. They had to become thorough Mussulmans.

3. To make Delegs' new name known to all the world, a coin, containing it in its legend, was to be struck for Ladakh in Kashmir. This coin was called *jau* (*jau* means "a little tea"), the name being taken from a similar Central Tibetan coin.

This *jau* is the first and only coin which the Western Tibetan empire has ever had. Trade was mostly carried on by barter only, the few coins which were occasionally used coming from the neighbouring districts. Cunningham, who examined the *jau* closely, gives the following reading of its legend :—Obverse: Mahmud Shah. Reverse : Butan (Tibet) Zarb (struck) sanat 878 (in the year 878).

4. Every encouragement was to be given to Mohammedanism in Ladakh, and a mosque erected at Leh. The great mosque which is now found at the upper end of the bazaar in Leh is not the first erected in Leh. There are two smaller ones which are said to be older. We do not know whether the great Balti village of Chushod near Leh was built after this war, or if the emigration from over-populated Baltistan had taken place already after Ali Mir's victory over the Ladakhis; at any rate, now the time of Mussulman propaganda begins for Ladakh, and on the accompanying map, the inroads of Mohammedanism into our country are shown.

5. Regarding the wool trade. When Kashmir was a province of the Mogul empire, and several Moguls built their beautiful summer residences on the shores of the Kashmiri lakes, great encouragement was given to the Kashmir industry of carpet-weaving. Most of the wool for these carpets came from the higher districts of Western Tibet, and thus the Kashmir industry depended largely on the wool trade with Ladakh. Delegs had to agree to the following points : [The fine wool of Tibet is to be sold to no country but Kashmir. The price shall be about seven battis for two rupees. To carry on the trade, four Kashmiris shall reside at Spitug and do the trading with the Kashmiris of Kashmir; but these four shall not be allowed to go down to Kashmir. On the other hand, no other Kashmiris, besides the four residing at Spitug, shall be allowed to go to the Tibetan highlands to buy the wool from the nomads.

6. A small annual tribute was to be sent to Kashmir, consisting of 18 piebald ponies, 18 pods of musk, and 18 white yak tails. (The latter were probably sold to Hindus for their temple ritual.) In exchange for these presents, the Nawab offered to send up to Ladakh annually 500 bags of rice, which is a delicacy in Western Tibet].

How glad was Delegs when the Nawab with his large army had left the country! He had just gone, when the Tibeto-Mongolians, who had been waiting on the Panggong lake, came out of their stronghold and dictated to Delegs what they wished him to agree to. They brought along with them a plenipotentiary of the Supreme Government at Lhasa, called Mipam wangpo,[1] and at Tingmogang the peace negotiations took place. Delegs had to agree to the following points :—

[1. The boundary between Central Tibet and Western Tibet is the Lhari stream, near the Panggong lake. Only in the domain of Menser in Guge may the Ladakhi king be his own master. Delegs protested against this sort of policy, but, apparently, without any effect. And the Lamas knew how to make the loss of the greater portion of his dominions palatable to Delegs. They simply declared it an offering to the religion of Buddha, by saying that the taxes of all those territories were to be used to defray the expenses of the sacrificial lamps and the reading of prayers in Tibet.] Although the name was sweet, the loss was bitter, for it meant the renunciation of the large provinces of Guge, Purang, Lowo, and Rutog; and after the peace of Tingmogang the history of the "small empire" begins, which lasted for a century and a half longer.

[2. Trade regulations with Lhasa. The King of Ladakh shall send once in three years a mission conveying presents to the clergy of Tibet. As regards presents to ordinary Lamas, the quantity is not fixed, but to the Dalai Lama's steward should be given thirty grammes of gold, ten weights of scent, six pieces of calico, and one piece of soft cotton cloth. The members of the mission shall receive daily rations and fodder for their animals free during their sojourn in Tibet. On the other hand, the Government trader of Tibet shall come every year with 200 loads of brick-tea, and nowhere but from Ladakh shall rectangular tea-bricks be sent across the frontier.]

All these trade regulations are in force to this day; only a few slight alterations in favour of Ladakh have been made. Bad as the affair had turned out for Delegs, his case would

1. On an inscription at Nyurla, this Lama had the title of viceroy. This shows that the authority of Delegs must have been badly shaken.

have been certainly worse, had he not called the Kashmiris to his assistance. In acknowledgement of that, probably, the chronicles conclude the account of him with these words : [The king, indeed, in all his doings had none to surpass him, and State and Church both made progress].

Songs of the Mongol siege of Basgo are well known at Basgo and Nyemo.

This is one of them :—

Looking towards the east from the city of Basgo;
Looking towards the east from the stronghold of Basgo;
On the field, called Pangkatse, of the king;
On the field, called Pangkatse, of the potentate,
There are three thousand five hundred little beds,
And three hundred and sixty little stones to regulate the irrigation of them.
As far as these fields reached the camp of the Mongol. the bad Hor;
As far as that reached the camp of the Mongol, the bad enemy.

10

The Quarrel for the Succession, about 1680-1780

NYIMA NAMGYAL, about 1680-1720, the son of Delegs namgyal. This is the first king of the "little empire," and the king during whose lifetime the quarrel began. His great wisdom is praised in the chronicles in this style :—

[In accordance with the rule, to act on the principles as described in the biographies of the ancient kings of the faith, he lauded the virtuous and suppressed evil-doers. In pronouncing judgement he never merely followed his own desires, but always, in the first place, consulted his staff-officers. He appointed elders of superior intelligence from every village to assist him. And such as wanted his decision in questions relating to field and house property he did not leave at the mercy of interlopers or partial advisers. But having instituted the council of state-officers and elders, he introduced the oath on the three symbols, and laid down the rule that first the primary origin of any dispute must be traced before the verdict was pronounced, and then found out what evidence is to be given. This edict surpasses in excellence any of those that were passed by all the dynastic kings of Tibet.]

After we have heard so much about Nyima's wisdom in pronouncing judgement, it will be of some interest to observe how a certain single case was decided. A document of such a procedure has been preserved at Kalatse, a translation of which I will now give. From very ancient times the Gongmapa family had held the highest position in the village, the eldest member of it being honoured with the title Wazir. It was apparently King Deldan namgyal who had made Dragchos chieftain of the village, without deposing the old Wazir. The people of Kalatse did not wish to have two superiors, and were in doubts which of the two was the person really to be respected. So King Nyima had to decide who was the true chieftain, and the following edict (on paper) is the document of his procedure :—

"This is the word of the protector of the earth, who is rich in power over men, Nyima namgyal, the god.

"It is proclaimed to all under my government in general, and to the elders of Kalatse in particular, as well as to the messengers who are sent up and down on errands either of peace or of war: Gangva gyatso, whose family has been Dragchos at Kalatse for three generations, on one occasion had a quarrel with Dondrub sodnam (the head of the Gongmapa family); they came to the court at Leh and quarrelled. The elders of Upper and Lower Ladakh, having carefully listened to the case, cast lots to find exactly the truth, and made the king swear an oath. Gangva gyatso won, and my oath is : I have shown kindness to Gangva gyatso, the Dragchos, from the days of my forefathers, and Dragchos has always done his work in a skilful way. Thus it is suitable for Dragchos to receive : the place of honour at festivals; the dish of honour; a share of the game from nine peasants, who must offer it in turns; a share of the harvest of straw and lucerne. As has been the former custom, I swear by the existence of the Namgyal tsemo hill and Yutur (unknown), and have made it clear that Dragchos receives authority as he had before. As my mercy also extends to letting him rank with the nobility, it is important that you noblemen neither despise him nor give him any commandments, but let him live in peace. Whoever, when seeing this letter, does not heed it, will be sternly brought to judgement. This must be understood by everybody. The petitioner is Sodnam Lundrub. Thus it is written on the 29th of the eighth month of the wood-monkey year (about 1705), at the Leh palace Pobrang tsemo."

What is of special interest in this case is that even by this king, who was particularly famous for his wisdom in pronouncing judgement, lots were cast. That made matters very easy indeed, and we wonder what sort of administration of justice may have been practised by other kings who were not particularly famous for their wisdom. Only the noblemen were allowed to enter into the presence of the king; other people had to speak to the king through one of them who was called the "petitioner." As is shown by the edict, Dragchos had to get his case stated by a petitioner also.

[During the reign of this king the first printing press was established in Ladakh, and after the blocks of six Lamaist books had been engraven, King Nyima distributed sacred Lamaist books among all the laity.] The art of printing had come to Tibet from China, where for many ages whole pages of books had been engraven on wooden tablets, from which they were printed on paper. Nyima's printing press is possibly still in existence. Some books are still printed at one of the temples below the castle.

[The most famous structure of King Nyima is a mani-wall at Choglamsa], above the bridge. Although it is considerably long, it is not of such imposing dimensions as the one built by Deldan, [He had also put up a huge prayer-wheel (Mani ten skor) of gold, silver, and copper (probably at Leh), and images of his favourite deity, of gold and silver. The monasteries of Central Tibet as well as Ladakh received presents from him.]

During the reign of Nyima namgyal, in 1715, the Jesuit Desideri passed through Leh on his way to Lhasa.

He was the first king, for a long time, under whom there was no warfare; and of this time of peace the chronicles say: [Amongst all the people there did not occur either strife, or robbery, or theft; it was a life passed in such happiness as that of a child with his fond mother.

King Nyima was married twice. His first wife died after she had given birth to a son, Lhachen Deskyong namgyal]. This sad event seems to have made an impression on the people; for the "Song of the girl of Sheh" shows us that people took a particular interest in little Prince Deskyong, and committed him to the care of his guardian deity. [King Nyima's second wife was Zizi katun of Purig. She bore him a son, Trashi namgyal, and a daughter, Trashi wangmo.

When Nyima became old, Deskyong namgyal was appointed king. But Zizi katun, his step-mother, wanted to get part of the kingdom for her son, Trashi namgyal, and, as she had always been kind to Deskyong, she persuaded him easily to give all Purig to Trashi. This was against the wishes of the state officials, who did not like to have a divided empire. They entered a petition that Trashi should either be made a Lama or live quietly at Tingmogang. When the quarrel became acute, old King Nyima seized the reins of the government once more and ruled for several years.]

Deskyong namgyal, about 1720-1740, was apparently an utterly insignificant ruler. [With his first wife, a princess of Lowo, he did not live in peace, until the two separated, on account of incompatibility of temper, soon after a son, Saskyong namgyal, had been born. Subsequently he married another wife, and a son, Puntsog namgyal, was born.] The government proper seems to have been in the hands of the queen-mother, Zizi katun, during all this time. Her most famous piece of diplomacy was the assassination of the chief of Kishtawar, who had married her daughter, Trashi wangmo. As might have been expected from the outset, this girl was kept in a zenana. [But when it was known in Ladakh that Trashi wangmo was not allowed to see the light of day, a Ladakhi was ordered to bring her back by fair means or foul. When the girl was being carried off, the chief and queen of Kishtawar, who were both very fond of her, said : "Let us also go to Ladakh !" But Zizi katun gave secret orders to this effect : "If the chieftain of Kishtawar should arrive here without being killed in some clever way beforehand, it might injure my son Trashi namgyal's rule over Purig ! See about this !" So, without the knowledge of the authorities of Ladakh, a servant of the queen went on this errand, and at a bridge on the frontier, between Kishtawar and Paldar, the servant, approaching the chieftain in the manner of one who has a petition, threw him into the water.]

Puntsog namgyal, about 1740-1760. Although he was the second son, he seized the government through the treachery of his mother. His elder brother, Saskyong namgyal, was shut up at Hemis as a Lama, much against his own will. Puntsog's realm was very small, as Purig was still in the hands of his uncle Trashi. Trashi brought the whole kingdom into great danger of a war with Kashmir, as he tyrannised not only over his Ladakhi subjects but also the Kashmir traders. As such a war not only endangered Ladakh but Central Tibet as well, the Dalai Lama resolved to regulate the political state of Ladakh, and sent as his plenipotentiary and peace-maker the great Lama Rigdzin tsewang norbu. This Lama was met on his arrival in Ladakh by King Trashi of Purig (probably because this gentleman had not exactly a good conscience), and all the princes and ministers of Ladakh were invited to a great council at the Hanle monastery. All agreed to the decisions and obligations imposed upon them by the "Saviour, the great Rigdzin." The results arrived at were : [Whatever the number of princes born at Ladakh castle may be, the eldest son only shall reign. The younger ones shall become Lamas at Trigtse, Spitug, and other monasteries; but there shall not be two kings.] If these resolutions had been carried into effect, we should certainly be ready to praise Rigdzin for his wisdom. But this great saviour had a very human side to his character : he did not wish to offend anybody; and although he was able to establish a very useful and sound principle, he was not the person to act according to it. There were a great number of rulers who ought to have been turned out at this juncture, but they all remained, and Rigdzin had a word of excuse for each of them. [The King of Zangskar was to remain as before, because he had to protect the frontier against Hindustan. Those members of the royal family who had received the castles of Zangla and Henasku with sixty or eighty peasants attached to them were also to remain as before, because their kingdoms were of little importance.] And uncle Trashi was to remain by all means, probably on account of his age. [Fortunately, Trashi namgyal had no children, and when he died Purig was united with Ladakh. In accordance with the decisions of the council, the son Tsewang namgyal (we are not told whether he was the son of Saskyong or Puntsog) was elected king. Puntsog and his mother equally divided the property in the Leh castle and appropriated it, and poor Saskyong had once more to enter the Hemis monastery.]

[*Tsewang namgyal II.*, about 1760-1780. Although by the great Rigdzin's settlement all the noblemen, the council of elders, and the merchants, first of all, but the whole empire as well, were rendered happy and contented], the new king, Tsewang, did not quite justify the amount of trouble the great Rigdzin had taken about his election.

Apparently, before the great saviour had left the country, there was considerable danger of war breaking out with Kashmir. It was averted only by a miracle. The water-courses below Leh were not regulated, and therefore [the Nawab sent messengers with the request that the plain below Leh should be cleared of water. On the occasion when the messengers had their audience, by a miracle tea was poured out from one silver teapot to all the men who took part in the banquet. The messengers believed and went home]. It is a pity we are not told what was the nature of the miracle; whether a little teapot held an enormous quantity or whether, the teapot had not to be lifted but flew about from one cup to the other to pour out the tea. At any rate, the superstitious Kashmiris thought it wisest to leave the Tibetans and their magic powers undisturbed.

As soon as the great Lama had left, Tsewang became troublesome, or, as the chronicles say, "the evil one entered his mind." [Messengers had been sent to Zangla in Zangskar to ask one of the princesses to become Tsewang's wife. They were probably a long time performing the journey, and before they returned Tsewang had fallen in love with a low-caste Bheda woman. The Zangla princess, who arrived soon after, knew well that she had not come to Ladakh to be made a fool of, and returned at once to her home. If the Ladakhis were not quite happy about their low-caste queen, they were even less pleased with Tsewang's further doings, viz. that he had one groom only for each 500 horses, and a lamp in grandest style at night. And when foolish Tsewang made the taxes payable three times in one year, a little revolution took place. In the eyes of the Ladakhis the source of all the offences was the low-caste queen. She was expelled from the palace, and the minister from the village of Stog, who was guilty in the same affair, had to go too. Then a Purig princess, Bhekyim wangmo, was asked to become queen, to which she agreed.]

Looking at the kings of this period, the thought cannot be avoided that the dynasty was on the decline. Not one of the kings of this chapter was great as a warrior, or as a politician, or organiser; they lived debauched lives, and women became occasionally the rulers of the state. Still, judging from the extraordinary multitude of documents on stone, referring to these kings, the people of Ladakh seem to have been wonderfully loyal and devoted. They praise their kings even for deeds of which they were quite innocent. Thus of Tsewang namgyal II., who never engaged in any war, it is said that his sword was "hot on the enemies of the country." A beautiful feeling of loyalty finds expression in the song about little Prince Deskyong, mentioned above, who had never known his own mother *(Ladakhi Songs*, No. XIV).

The Song of the Girl of Sheh

On the hill in the back there is the chorten of white crystal ;
In the front there is the lake, blue like a turquoise.
On the shore flowers are in bloom.
They grow in my fatherland together with its future.
On the shore large yellow flowers are in bloom.
In the castle of Sheh the milk (of abundance) flows.
On the high summit there lives
The eloquent god of the summit.
Wherever our gracious prince goes,
Oh God, protect his life !
To Deskyong namgyal, the (future) lord of men
Give blessing during his lifetime.
The Lama who is loved by the girl,
Is beautiful like a picture of the gods in the temple.
The Lama who is loved by Zangmo,
Is beautiful like a picture of the gods in the temple.
With pure and holy words
Bring offerings to God !
With pure and holy words
Give alms to the poor !

11

The Last Two Kings, about 1780-1834

TSEWANG NAMGYAL II. had two sons from Bhekyim wangmo. The name of the eldest was *Tsestan namgyal*, about 1780-1790; that of the younger one Tsepal (dondrub) namgyal. According to the resolution of the Council of Hanle, Tsestan was made king, and Tsepal had to enter the Hemis monastery.

It appeared as if the dynasty was making a new start; for Tsestan was more of a character than many of the kings before him. The chronicles describe him thus : [His personal appearance was like that of a god. He was diligent, and obtained proficiency in Tibetan grammar and mathematics, Persian letters and speech, Kashmir speech, and other such languages. He also knew well how to govern. He was devout, and knew the duties of kings. Before the enemy he was fearless. His solicitude for the welfare of his subjects was exceedingly great. Between himself and others he knew no difference].

Although he had no opportunity to distinguish himself in a great war, he had opportunity to fight occasionally on frontier expeditions. At Kalatse there is a document in existence, of a few years after him, from which we learn that private individuals were at liberty in time of peace to go on raiding expeditions to Baltistan. The document states the number of Baltis killed, and gives the reward (a piece of desert land) which the raider (the Dragchos of Kalatse) received.

His ability to govern was evidenced in his regulation of the taxes. [As, thus far, there had been no principle regulating taxes and revenue, he made a rule that henceforth taxes should be raised only in accordance with the income, measure for measure.

In memory of his father he built the Skyin mani ringmo, the second largest mani-wall in the country, with chortens at either end, of the great Namgyal and Jangchub types.] It resembled very much the long mani-wall built by Deldan namgyal, and is situated a little above Deldan's mani-wall. It stretches from there towards Leh. Tsestan was a great polo-player. There is a song still known, according to which he used to play on the polo-ground of the Murtse garden, below Leh. Popular tradition says that once his pony got shy, ran away with him, and threw him off. In this accident he is said to have lost one eye.

[The mani-wall was his last work, for in a neighbouring district some "defect" became apparent, and in consequence of want of merit in the people (they had apparently not prayed *Om mani padme hums* enough) an epidemic of smallpox broke out, and Tsestan died in his twenty-fourth year at Leh in the Karzo garden. Then a great Lama of Hemis, who once had received rich presents from the king, performed the funeral rites in grand style.]

[Tsestan died without leaving any children, and therefore his brother *Tsepal namgyal*, about 1790-1841, of Hemis, was induced to turn layman and was invested with royal power.] He inherited from his brother not only the kingdom but also his wife. Lama though he was, he had always been considered second husband to the queen ; and, indeed, the Tibetan custom of polyandry makes it very easy for the Lamas to surround themselves with a halo of a pure life and yet to indulge in the pleasures of less holy men. In character Tsepal was the opposite to Tsestan. He loved an easy life, and was lazy in every respect. He never went to battle, although he had plenty of opportunity to do so. [In judgement, he regarded the faces and riches of men.]

Besides, he seems to have inherited the taint of madness from his father; for many strange things are told about him. [The private servants in the palace had to promise daily not to sleep at night. The king also did not sleep at night. He rose when the sun grew hot. In the morning, when washing his hands, he required twelve or thirteen basins full of cold and hot water. When he travelled about in the provinces he went at night, and then with lamps and torches. The King of Zangskar and the Purig kalon (minister) he kept in prison.

With the men of the old regime he did not agree. This was not so much due to his extravagance as to the fact that he made the new-fashioned servants that stood before him governors of the palace, and took counsel with them. In spite of this foolish sort of government, for some time the country was in a flourishing state; everybody lived in affluence; and such "works as were all and one on the side of virtue" enjoyed peace and happiness. This blessed state was due to the activity of the powerful minister, Tsewang dondrub, the brother-in-law of the king. But when Tsepal took the privy seal from the minister to his own palace, Tsewang dondrub seems to have been offended, for he disappears from the pages of history.]

In the reign of this king falls also Moorcroft's visit to Ladakh, 1820-1822. This event is described in the chronicles in this manner : [At that time, having passed through Kulu and Lahoul, the *bara Sahib* (great Lord), and the *chota Sahib* (little Lord), with great wealth, came to Leh. They gave all sorts of rich presents to the noblemen of Ladakh and many others. "We must see the king!" they said, and all that was said in reply was: "What evil there is in Indians one cannot know!" An audience for consultation was refused for several months, but at last they saw the king. They presented a variety of things, but the best were a penknife, scissors, and a gun. They said: "We have come to see the way in which your ministers and people behave, and your majesty's wisdom; and as there is a likelihood of this country being conquered, if we built a tower (fort) here it would prove useful to the king." The king and his ministers, in considering the case, said: "If they build a fort, no one knows what means of doing harm it may be!" and did not allow them to build it. Then they gave the king a letter in a box and said: "Accept this; it may cure the king's mind!" They stayed throughout both summer and winter, and departed. These were the first European sahibs who came].

How much Tsepal must have regretted, about twelve years after, that he had despised the friendship of the English! How useful it would have been to support him against all kinds of external enemies! When it was too late this visit of the sahibs was remembered, and the assistance of the English solicited, as the course of events will show. The principal reason why Tsepal did not accept the assistance of the British was hardly his mistrust, but his extreme laziness, and his desire to remain undisturbed. He had apparently got a liking for the meditative life of the monks, and would have been best pleased had he been left at Hemis. His gross carelessness became most evident when the people of Kulu and Lahoul, who had once been the subjects of the Ladakhi emperors, came on raiding expeditions to his own country.

[Thereupon the army of Kulu invaded Spiti, and after having destroyed the villages, and carried away all the property, they returned home. The Ladakhis petitioned Tsepal that he should wage a war of revenge, but he said: "You have not tried your best!" and punished them.

Later on, the people of Kulu and Lahoul conspired against Zangskar, and laid waste the castle of Spadum and the central districts. They stole ponies and yaks and whatever there was of value, and again returned home. But now, under the command of a general of Paldar, an army, chiefly of Lower Ladakhis (Rastanpas), went against the enemy. All the Lahoul villages from Spadum to Garing (Aring seems to be a mistake) were destroyed. Throughout Lahoul and the central districts (of Kulu) they fought; and although afterwards peace was made, King Tsepal said: "You Zangskar people have not yet tried your best!" and punished them.

One year later, a Mande and Waran army (from Kishtawar) came and devastated Upper Zangskar, up to Dung ring. They burnt the villages with fire; whatever of wealth and cattle they got they carried back with them.] From all these notes it looks as if the Ladakhi kingdom of those days had got quite a name among its neighbours for being an easy prey to conquerors. And in course of time its fame may have travelled as far as Jammu.

[Although the land had to suffer so much, the king did not perceive it, and he never asked whether his subjects fared well or ill; he took an interest only in what concerned his own pocket. At that time the royal treasure had increased so much that something had to be done with it, and the king decided to use the money for building purposes. The first work he undertook was the new palace at Stog, a village opposite Leh, of which people say that it is "one dress colder" than Leh. (Difference in climate is in this country expressed by the greater or smaller number of clothes which are worn one above the other.) The other palace built by Tsepal is the palace of the crown prince at Leh, above the Chanraszigs (Avalokitesvara) monastery. Tsepal's eldest son was Tsewang rabstan, and as he was on the point of being married to a princess of a province in Central Tibet (Lhagyari), the palace was built for the couple; but it is not quite clear whether it was built by the father of the bride or of the bridegroom. In the end, however, through some misfortune in Tibet, the princess could not be asked to come there. Besides these two palaces, Tsepal erected a number of idols, mostly made of silver: a Vajrapani (Phyagna rdorje) with a silver head, the figure being of the same size as the king, because this deity was his patron; a figure of the saint Guru Padma od bar, made of thirteen maunds of silver; at Sheh a Tsepagmed (a symbol?), made of seven maunds of silver; a white Tara (sgrolma), who since the days of Gyal katun was supposed to be incarnated in the Ladakhi queens, of nine maunds of silver; and a chorten of silver, with ornaments in gold, copper, and precious stones.] Most of these silver images were probably carried off later on by the Dogras.

The eldest son of Tsepal, Tsewang rabstan namgyal, seems to have died soon; for the interest of the chronicles is now turned towards Tsepal's second son, Chogsprul namgyal, who had a will of his own when he was a child. Apparently to please his father (the "master of perfect insight," Lama Yangdzin ngapa, discovered that the prince was an incarnation of the great Lama, Bhilva dorje, who had flourished during the reign of Tsewang namgyal II., and then the boy stayed at Hemis and Chemre. Having thus become so important a personage, he found it difficult to obey father and mother. Fortunately, there was still one person whose word he heeded; this was the queen's own steward, Sodnam wangchug. The queen, his mother, who was apparently very proud of her son, travelled about with him in Nubra, Purig, and Ladakh, never remaining at one and the same place. "It is for the prince's amusement!" she said, and they passed their time, both day and night, with dancing and singing. When the boy was old enough (presumably sixteen or seventeen years) the king and ministers attempted to induce him to marry, for the sake of the dynasty, but he would not. He replied: "I have to be at Hemis!" and would not relent. But as there was no other son, the king, ministers, lords, council of elders and the stewards of the head Lamaseries interceded with him; and in order to preserve the dynasty, he consented and married the younger daughter of the minister Tsewang dondrub, Skalzang rolma by name. Having once tasted the sweetness of matrimony, he married yet another lady, Tsunmo palskyid, of Pashkyum, and yet a third, Zora Katun. It was in a horse-year (1834) that he took these three wives, and it was in the same horse-year that Zorawar, with the Dogra army, arrived at Kartse.)

By this time Tsepal had grown old, and although the chronicles have not told us much to enlist our admiration, still, in the memory of the people, Tsepal lives as the ideal patriarchal King of Ladakh. As he was the last independent king, all the virtues of his predecessors were believed to have been united in him. From this point of view we can best understand the description of the state of the country before the outbreak of the Dogra war, as it is given by Tsebstan of Kalatse: "At the time of the father-king (Tsepal), the following were his subjects: the people who dwelt between the Zoji Pass, Ladar, Shedula, and Polong drandra, they all were his subjects. Besides the father-king, no one was allowed to say anything here. To say 'Salaam' to the king there came from Kashmir a man called Malik annually, and together with him about one hundred ponymen. In reply to this the Ladakhi king sent with a man from Kalatse, called Dragchos dondrub, various products of Ladakh as a present; for instance, a horse, a yak, a sheep, a goat, a dog, and also more valuable things. (This refers to the peace of Tingmogang, 1647, the Sikhs taking the place of the Moguls.)

"The head steward of the king's household was the minister Puntsog rabstan of Nyemo; the royal cook was a man of the house 'cook' at Wanla; the royal butcher was Stobdan of the house 'butcher' at Alchi, and another man in Rubchu. All the grain for the royal household had to be brought from Nubra, and a nobleman, called Standzin, had the care of it. The needful butter had to be provided by a man from Zangskar. Besides this the peasants had no taxes to pay, and there was no unpaid forced labour.

"When the king's merchants went to Lhasa (every three years, according to the peace of Tingmogang), every village had to send one man for the caravan. This man received two *jaus* (about sixpence) from every peasant in the village, as wages for his journey. For the same caravan every village had to give two hides, but the larger villages three. They were used to wrap up the goods.

"Toll had to be paid by the Kashmiris, Yarkandis, and the Lahoul traders on entering Ladakh; but it was not asked of the people of Purig, Baltistan, and Tibet.

"Several villages were in debt to the king, and all their fields had been given to the king as security. On the day when the king's son (probably Chogsprul) was made assistant king to his father, all the debts were remitted. That act of the king was very much liked by the people."

During this time of innocent thoughtlessness minister Ngorub Standzin composed his hymn in honour of King Tsepal. Of this poet we shall hear more later on. The hymn is found in *Ladakhi Songs*, No. I.

Through perfect good fortune
The happiness containing garden Karzo,
Not being built, came into existence by itself.
It is the house of the gods and the sun.
Having in the zenith of the clear sky
Sun and moon like umbrellas, so it arose.
It is a wonderfully pleasing sight ;
It is like a fine room with pairs of pillars.
Within, on a lion's throne,
Sits Nyatri tsanpo's family.
That is the king of faith, Tsepal, with mother and son.
May their feet on the lotus stand one hundred cycles of years !
On this magnificent high nut-tree
Male and female birds sing melodious songs.

Underneath, the youths. having gathered
Sing a song of happiness and welfare.

"This song of praise was written by the Leh minister, Ngorub Standzin, in the fine castle within the Karzo garden."

12

The Fall of the Western Tibetan Empire, 1834-1840

DURING the first decades of the nineteenth century the most important power of North India, except that of the English East India Company, was the fast-rising empire of the Sikhs, with Ranjit Singh, "The Lion of the Punjab," at its head. When this great warrior conquered Kashmir, in 1819, he was assisted by Gulab Singh, the Maharajah of Jammu, the head of the Dogra tribe. The latter prince, although at first an ally of the Sikhs, felt more and more inclined to take the side of the English, when, after Ranjit Singh's death, an estrangement between the Sikhs and the English made itself more and more felt. As already in 1834 he considered himself the friend of the British, he did not wish to start on any enterprise before having ascertained the consent of the East India Company. Thus, before his intended conquest of the Ladakhi kingdom, he made a confidential inquiry, whether the company would have any objection to such a campaign. As the English had no reason to interfere with it, they are by certain critics looked upon as participators in the atrocities and cruelties of the Ladakhi wars; but, I think, without reason. We must not forget that in the year 1834 the districts of the Ladakhi kingdom were practically unknown ground to Europeans. Before Moorcroft, no European had known much about the existence of the kingdom;[1] and twelve years after him much more was not yet known. At any rate, there was no reason why the English should have felt responsible for the fate of the Western Tibetan State. It was much the same as if, forty years ago, the Sultan of Uganda had

1. The short visits of the Jesuits to Ladakh had been forgotten.

asked the English if they had any objection to his waging war against the Unyamwezi.

That the Dogra chief had directed his attention to Ladakh was probably due to the revelation of Tsepal's careless policy. Still, although successful raiding expeditions had been conducted into the frontier provinces of the country, the direct conquest of the kingdom was not without great risks, and of these the Dogra chief was probably aware. The severe cold of the climate was certain to reduce the usefulness of his Indian warriors, at least during the winter months; the barrenness of the country prohibited the mobilisation of a large army. Lack of knowledge of the roads made slow progress advisable. Still, in certain respects the Dogras were superior to the Ladakhis from the outset. Their participation in several Indian wars had taught them tactics and discipline. Their equipment was up to date, whilst that of the Ladakhis was several centuries behind. And they had an experienced leader, whilst the Ladakhis had none. But one of the greatest advantages the Dogras obtained by surprising the Ladakhi kingdom at the time of deepest peace.

The following account is compiled from three histories of the Dogra war, which are only in a few instances, and on minor points, in conflict with each other; but as they all narrate different incidents of the same war, it is not at all easy to arrange them in chronological order. The first is the official Ladakhi history, as we find it in the chronicles.[1] The second are the personal reminiscences of a Ladakhi warrior, called Tsebstan, who died at Kalatse in 1905, about ninety years old. The third is the account of the Dogra colonel, Basti Ram, written at General Sir Alexander Cunningham's request in 1846, and published in his *Ladak*. In this account the succession of events is perhaps the most correct.

As the Dogras could not march through Kashmir, which then was the territory of the Sikhs, Gulab Singh sent his general Zorawar, with about 10,000 men, through Kishtawar, from whence the Ladakhi province of Purig, in particular the

1. In the following pages it was found impossible to mark passages taken from the chronicles as before.

possessions of the Tri Sultan of Kartse, was soon reached. On the 16th of August 1834, Zorawar was opposed for the first time by a Ladakhi force of about 5000, which had been mobilised in haste, and placed under the command of the young minister of Stog, a dashing boy of only eighteen years. At Sanku, the Ladakhis had entrenched themselves on a hill, and defended it with much vigour for a full day. Unfortunately, with their very old matchlocks, they could not do much harm to the storming Dogras. Although the latter exposed themselves very much more than the Ladakhis, only six or seven Dogras were killed, while the Ladakhi losses are given by Basti Ram as thirty killed and as many wounded. At that time, the eccentric Dr Henderson was in Leh. He was asked by the king to prepare an allegiance with the English ; but as that was not in his power, he was imprisoned at Leh, and kept there for several months.

After the battle of Sanku the Ladakhis marched during the night across the Russi Pass to Shergol, where they halted for eight days. Thus the most important fortress of the district, Kartse, the seat of the Tri Sultans, remained in the hands of the Dogras, and they further improved their holds on the country by building a fort at Suru, and taking the neighbouring unoccupied fort of Shagkar. Taxes were levied on the peasants of all the villages which had been taken possession of. Every peasant had to pay four rupees.

Leaving thirty-five men in the castle of Suru, the Dogra army moved down the Suru River. First of all Langkartse was taken, and by and by, fighting occasionally, but never with the whole Ladakhi force, the Dogra army arrived in the plain of Pashkyum. By this time the Ladakhis were in the expectation of reinforcements. The old king had sent his ministers, Ngorub Standzin and Bangkapa, to mobilise all those districts which had not yet sent any warriors, and now a force of about 4000 men was advancing towards Pashkyum. Apparently, before the arrival of this army, the young minister of Stog attacked the Dogras, and the fortunes of the day were almost on the side of the Ladakhis, when their brave young captain was suddenly struck by a musket ball and died. This was for the Ladakhis, superstitious as they are, the signal for a general flight. They fled in all directions, but most of them across the

Pashkyum bridge, towards Mulbe and Shergol. After having passed the bridge, they had sense enough left to break it down. But the Dogras knew another method of crossing the river. They did so on inflated skins, and in the pursuit killed many Ladakhis and made many more prisoners. Then the Dogras directed their attention to the Pashkyum castle, but found it empty, as the chief had fled to the castle of Sod, a little north of Kargil. Before Sod a battery was placed, and after ten day's firing Basti Ram was sent to the attack, and seized the castle and a numerous garrison. But the number of captives in the battles of Pashkyum and Sod (6000), as given by Basti Ram, is a gross exaggeration. There may have been 600. The fugitive Ladakhi army had arrived meanwhile before the two new leaders, and told them terror inspired stories of the greatness and armament of the Dogra army.

But winter began to make itself felt in the Dogra camp, and, in spite of his successes, Zorawar would very much have liked to end the campaign and march back to Kishtawar, at any rate to spend the winter there. But he knew very well that he could not come before his sovereign, Gulab Singh, without a present of a considerable sum of money. And up to the present he had not got anything, besides the few rupees of the peasants round about Kartse. So he levied taxes on the peasants of the Pashkyum district, and then sent an envoy to open negotiations with the Ladakhis. He offered to go back, if a sum of 15,000 rupees was paid to him promptly. That was exactly what the Ladakhi generals wished to hear, and a messenger on horseback was at once sent with a letter to King Tsepal. Tsepal, as well as the council of noblemen, was pleased with the offer, and the sum would have been paid at once if one of the queens, as the chronicles tell, had not interfered, and prohibited the payment of the sum, which, in her eyes, was money thrown away. Thus the messenger, when he arrived back in the Ladakhi camp, brought nothing but a letter in which the two generals received orders to bring Zorawar's head and hands to Leh, otherwise they would lose their own heads.

If the Ladakhis had not had such unenterprising leaders they would have made use of the extreme cold of the winter, and might have been able to annihilate the Dogra army. A small attempt they actually made, and the fact that the success they actually attained was not utilised can only be comprehended on the ground of the incompetency of their generals. When the Dogra envoys returned to the Ladakhi camp, to receive the 15,000 rupees, as they hoped, they were, as Basti Ram tells, treacherously seized and thrown from the bridge at Darkyed. Not only that, but minister Bangkapa, by a circuitous route attacked the Dogras in the rear, made some prisoners, who were at once bound and thrown into the river, and compelled the Dogras to go back to Langkartse, near Kartse. Now would have been the time for powerful attacks on the Dogras. Instead, the foolish Ladakhis left the enemy unmolested for about four months.

During this time they seem to have tried to increase their army by further mobilisation. The Ladakhi empire never had a standing army. Since the introduction of fire-arms, which had taken place at any rate before the reign of Sengge rnam rgyal, under whom fire-arms are mentioned for the first time, every household was furnished with a matchlock. This old weapon and a certain supply of powder had to be kept in readiness for times of war. When the call to arms was sent round the country, one man with the matchlock had to come from every house, carrying on his back provisions to last him for a whole month (chiefly parched grain) and blankets for the night. This load was so heavy, as Tsebstan tells us, that the mobility of the army was considerably impeded by it. Artillery there was none. Cavalry it would have been easy to raise, but it was not of much use in the mountainous country. The whole army may have amounted to 15,000 men—at the utmost, perhaps, 20,000.

Now that the winter was almost over, the Ladakhis decided in a long consultation to make use of the heavy snowfalls, to which the Dogras certainly were not accustomed, as they thought, and to attack them at Langkartse. If there was anything that impeded the Dogras, it was not the heavy snow of the late spring but the extreme cold of mid-winter, which deprived them of the use of their fingers and thus also of their superior arms. Now their benumbed fingers had thawed and the deep snow made itself felt at least as much to the Ladakhis, with their heavy loads as to the Dogras. When the Ladakhi army arrived before Langkartse nobody knew what he was to do, as there was no agreement between the leaders. The Dogras watched the endless consultations which apparently led to no result, and saw the whole army after all settling down to prepare the evening meal. The Dogras knew by this time that they had nothing to fear from this sort of an enemy. They attacked the Ladakhis, and, as these did not receive any clear orders from their officers, they hurried away from their teapots and fled. During their flight, however, they made use of their arms, and the Dogras lost, according to their own statement, three leaders and twenty men killed, and fifty to sixty wounded; but there may have been many more. Still, the greatest loss was inflicted on the Ladakhis by the snow, which they had believed to be on their own side. A party of 400 fleeing Ladakhis broke through a snow-bridge over the river and were drowned. Two hundred, as the Dogras say, were made prisoners, among them Ngorub Standzin, the general without any initiative.[1]

The Ladakhi army retreated as far as Mulbe, and the Dogras moved down to Pashkyum for the second time. When the Ladakhis heard of this movement, they retired still further towards Leh. Thus both armies were moving in the same direction, the Ladakhis being generally two days in the front of the Dogras. Those Purig chiefs who had been kept in prison by Tsepal some time before, served as guides to the Dogras. Why the Ladakhis did not break down all the bridges during their retreat is difficult to understand. When the Dogras arrived at Kharbu, the people of Lamayura felt much fear, and, to save their property, they sent a pony and some money as a present to Zorawar, who was well pleased, and sent a soldier to Lamayuru as a safeguard. When the army arrived at that place the people of Tea Tingmogang became frightened. They sent two horses with some money, and also received a safeguard. When the Dogras had got as far as Nyurla (*snyungla*) they were met by embassies from the villages of Saspola, Alchi, Nyemo, and

1. From Tsebstan's accounts it looks almost as if the young minister had died in this battle. But it is more probable that he died before, as the chronicles have it.

Likir, who all brought presents and did homage to Zorawar, and he promised to protect them.

At Basgo, the first meeting of Zorawar with King Tsepal took place, and it appears as if the peace negotiations had been practically finished at Basgo, and that Zorawar went up to Leh only, as he said, "to see the capital." When the Wazir came to Leh he had only a very small detachment of soldiers with him as a guard ; but he had given secret orders that more soldiers, always in twos, should come up after him ; and shortly a considerable number were assembled in Leh. Basti Ram gives a different explanation of practically the whole Dogra army being at Leh. He tells that Zorawar made a present of 100 rupees in a bag to the crown-prince, Chogsprul, which he swung round the young man's head. The latter mistook this act of goodwill for an attack, and drew his sword. Then also the bystanding Dogras drew their swords. Tsepal went down on his knees and clasped Zorawar's feet, and there was a little scene, until matters had been explained. This little episode is given as the reason why the Dogra army came up to Leh.

The second part of the peace negotiations took place in the Karzo garden, where Zorawar had his tent. Zorawar's first act was to restore the whole kingdom to Tsepal, which the latter accepted with much pleasure and great respect. As, however, the kingdom was henceforth to be considered a vassal-state of the Dogra kingdom of Jammu, Tsepal was asked to pay an annual tribute of 20,000 rupees. Besides, he was ordered to pay on the spot 50,000 rupees towards the expenses of the war. As so much money could not possibly be procured in Leh, it was arranged that only 37,000 rupees were to be paid at once, in cash and jewels, 6,000 after one month, and 7,000 after four months. The Ladakhi chronicles give only 9,000 as the annual tribute, and do not mention the war indemnity at all. But it is more probable that Basti Ram's higher figures are correct.

After a stay of four months, Zorawar left Leh, and marched back to Lamayura. The war would perhaps have been at an end now, if the Sikhs had not grudged the Dogras the conquest of Ladakhi. But at the instigation of Mihan Singh, the Sikh Governor of Kashmir, the Ladakhis revolted again and again against their powerful masters. The first Ladakhi who listened to the promises of Mihan Singh was the chief of Sod, whose castle had been bombarded. When Zorawar was in Leh, the chief of Sod marched against the Dogra fort at Suru, captured it, and put the small garrison to death. Of this event Zorawar heard when he was at Lamayura. He marched at once to Suru, where he surprised the Ladakhis and seized thirteen, who were hanged. As, however, his thirst for revenge was not yet quenched, he promised a reward of 50 rupees per head for any others of the chief of Sod's force. The peasants, who were anxious to get their 50 rupees, soon accused 200 men of having partaken in this chief's insurrection. They were all beheaded without trial.

Then the Wazir, Zorawar, marched in ten days to Zangskar, the king of which place promised to pay a tax of 3½ rupees for each house. After all this had been accomplished the Wazir went, apparently, to Jammu, to report his success to his master, Gulab Singh.

During the winter (apparently 1835-36) King Tsepal listened to the suggestions of Mihan Singh, the Governor of Kashmir, and began to prepare a revolution against the Dogra rule. He closed the roads to the trade, and imprisoned and tortured the Dogra representative, Munshi Daya Ram, who was stationed at Leh. Before the Ladakhis had done much more, Zorawar arrived with an army at Chemre, above Leh, which he had reached after passing through Zangskar and Shang, and King Tsepal, who had not even a small army at his disposal, hastened to the bridge at Chushod, where he humbly bowed before Zorawar and expressed his sorrow for what had happened. The Wazir said: "Although we conquered your country with only 10,000 men, we did not place a single man of our own over your districts; and this is the way you show your gratitude!" The king was much ashamed, but he may have thought, as we do, that the Dogras' mild treatment of the conquered dynasty was not so much due to their sense of mercy as to their hope of getting more money out of the country. The heir-apparent of Ladakh, Prince Chogsprul, who probably was implicated in the rising, fled on Zorawar's arrival through Spiti to Lahoul. As popular tradition says, he hoped to gain the assistance of the English against the Dogras. Moorcroft's visit was suddenly remembered, and the Ladakhis still assert that in a talk with some European sahibs Chogsprul received the promise of military help. But about all this there is no certainty whatever; nobody even knows who the sahibs were. After the interview Chogsprul went back to Spiti, and died there.

Old Tsepal had to accompany the Wazir to Leh, where the balance of 13,000 rupees for the expenses of the war was demanded. They had not yet been paid, nor was Tsepal in the possession of any cash now. It was paid by taking the property of the royal ladies. But there were the additional expenses of the new war, and to meet them Tsepal's minister offered all sorts of things, which were accepted, as nothing better could be got out of the country.

But the Wazir had to arrange matters on a new principle. Tsepal could not be trusted with the government any longer; he was dismissed, and received the village of Stog, together with the taxes of about sixty peasants. Then arose the question who was to take his place? Chogsprul had died, and a Dogra was hardly able to manage the Ladakhis satisfactorily. Zorawar had learnt to know a Ladakhi who appeared to be a trustworthy man. This was Dragchos, the first man of Kalatse. He was asked to accept the responsibility for all Ladakh. However, Dragchos, who had always been a true and faithful servant of his old king, looked upon the new and high position offered him as an act of infidelity against his former master, and said: "Until now have I been a servant of the King of Ladakh, and have received ample food and drink from him. I shall not now revolt against him. Zorawar was much displeased with this proof of loyalty, and Dragchos was taken to Jammu at the next opportunity, and nobody has ever heard of him since.

Then Zorawar directed his attention to Ṅgorub Standzin, the Ladakhi general—a relation of the old king—who had been made a prisoner, and found him at once ready to accept the dignity of a king of Ladakh. Ngorub Standzin's career was as follows : First, an official of the king, who wrote poetry in honour of his master; next, a general of the Ladakhi army, who through his want of initiative and his half-heartedness was mainly the cause of the downfall of the empire; then, a prisoner of the Dogras; and now suddenly king of Ladakh. He seems to have been one of those who easily impress others, especially the mob; for there is a song still known about his wedding, in which much is made of him. Zorawar built a fort at Leh, and placed 300 soldiers in it. Then he went to Jammu, taking along with him Ngorub Standzin's son and several other people as hostages. On the way down, when passing by the palatial residence of Tingmogang, Zorawar emptied this treasure-house of the Ladakhi kings and destroyed it. The manifold articles which he had received as the Ladakhi contribution towards the expenses of the war were probably not considered sufficient. Presumably the castle of Basgo was destroyed and plundered at the same time.

When Zorawar was in Jammu a little revolt took place in Zangskar, and Basti Ram received orders to quell it with 1500 men. He did so, and left a garrison of twenty men at the fort of Chatgarh, on the south-western frontier.

Gulab Singh was not pleased to hear that Ngorub Standzin had been placed on the throne of Ladakh. Zorawar replied that he belonged to the royal family, but that he would be deposed if Gulab Singh preferred it. A reason for deposing the new king was soon found, for the news was brought in that another revolt had taken place in Zangskar, and that the garrison of twenty men at Chatgarh had been annihilated. Although it is very improbable that Ngorub Standzin had any hand in this affair, he was called the originator of it.

Zorawar started with 3000 infantry. The swollen state of the rivers made their progress difficult. But they arrived before Chatgarh, and took it by storm. Their losses were fifteen, whilst those of the enemy were twenty dead and twenty to thirty prisoners. All the prisoners had their ears and noses cut off.

When the Dogras went from Chatgarh to Spadum, the capital of Zangskar, the cold was so severe that twenty-five men died in the snow, and many others lost their hands and feet. Therefore, before proceeding any farther, it was thought necessary to stay there for two months, to await pleasanter weather. When, after that time, Ngorub Standzin heard that the Wazir was advancing towards Leh, he left all his royal dignity behind and fled to Spiti, although the enemy numbered only 1000. Whether he actually had a bad conscience, or whether he was only afraid of slander, cannot be decided. But no favourable interpretation was put upon his flight. He was followed, and seized in Spiti. Then he was locked up in the Leh prison.

Now old King Tsepal was reinstated on the terms of 23,000 rupees annual tribute. Then the Wazir went to Jammu and stayed there for one year. At the end of that time he had once more to come to Ladakh to seize imprisoned Ngorub Standzin and several others who had been plotting against old Tsepal. They were all transported to Jammu.

The following is a passage from the song of Prince Chogsprul's flight :—

The sun is rising, the warm sun of the East;
He is rising on the summit of the good place of threefold happiness.
May the pure rays of the sun fall on the fatherland where I was born !
May the pure rays of the sun fall on the great town of Leh with its three courts of government !
When I, a boy, lived in my fatherland, I was surrounded by servants, inside and outside the palace.
When Chogsprul lived in the great town of Leh, the number of his servants was like the stars of heaven.
When I, a boy, went to a foreign country, I was alone with my horse.
When Chogsprul went to Spiti, we were only one man and one horse.
When we went across all the large and little plains, I was so thirsty that I humbly prayed for water.
When I, a boy, was still in my fatherland, I had always a pair of teapots, like the sun and moon.
Then I, a boy, went to sleep under a cedar-tree...

13

The Conquest of Baltistan, 1841

DURING the winter of 1840 to 1841 the Ladakhis were again in a state of excitement, because a man from Purig, called Sukamir, had issued a call-to-arms to the whole country. Several other influential men of Purig had joined Sukamir in issuing similar orders, and an army was being formed in the vicinity of Leh. Although old Tsepal did nothing to encourage the insurrection, he did just as little to stop it. Before the movement had grown sufficiently to become dangerous to the Dogras, Zorawar, the man who always arrived in the country at the wrong time for the Ladakhis, entered Leh at the head of a large army. The Ladakhi army which was being collected could no longer be concealed from the Dogras, and therefore they tried to deceive them. They said that they were a body of petitioners who had come to greet Zorawar and tell him their different woes. Zorawar was equal to the occasion, and advised them to leave their leaders with him, and the rest to go home. In this way Zorawar got Sukamir and several other Purig leaders in his power, and the hostile army melted away of itself. After a few days the Ladakhis were cross-examined with regard to the originators of the revolt, and Sukamir was recognised as its instigator.

Zorawar ordered the executioner to come with his sword, and to place a pot filled with butter over a fire. Then, whilst Zorawar was abusing his victim, the executioner was ordered to cut off Sukamir's right hand and to dip the stump at once into the boiling butter. (This is the Dogra way of stopping excessive bleeding.) Then the executioner had also to cut off

Sukamir's tongue. To warn the Ladakhis against following other evil advisers, Zorawar ordered Sukamir's hand to be exhibited in public on a pole at the Kalatse bridge. The hand arrived there all right, and was placed during the night in the rest-house. But a cat stole it, and the peasants of Kalatse greatly feared that all their hands might be cut off, as a punishment for their neglect. Fortunately an old Lama had died only a few days before. His hand was cut off and fastened on the top of the pole at the bridge, where it served its purpose as well as the other would have done.

Then Zorawar had a new idea to keep the Ladakhis from intriguing against the rule of the Dogras. If they formed part of the Dogra army on a new expedition, it would give them something to do. Therefore Zorawar decided on an expedition against Baltistan. This time, too, he had a pretext to wage war against that country. The old chief of Skardo, Ahmed Shah, had excluded his eldest son, Muhamad Shah, from the succession, in favour of his second son. Muhamad Shah fled to Zorawar, and asked for his assistance in obtaining the throne. Zorawar was very glad of the opportunity, and resolved to give Ahmed Shah a lesson concerning the most natural law of succession.

The Ladakhi half of the army was placed under the command of their old general, Bangkapa, and had orders to enter Baltistan by Hanu and the Chorbat Pass. This portion of the army never came within sight of the enemy, and reached Skardo in course of time without having fired a bullet. With this portion of the army also old King Tsepal, whom Zorawar did not wish to leave alone in Ladakh, probably had to march.

The Dogra and Purig portion of the army started from Kargil, and went along the Dras River and the Indus. The Dogras had crossed the Indus and were on the right bank; then the Indus had to be crossed once more, as the road continued on the left bank, and the Baltis, after having marched across, had broken down the bridge. Thus the Dogras tried to find a road on the right bank, to get round the many precipices and empty gaps. At the beginning Mir Nidhan Singh was dispatched with 5000 men on this errand. But the Baltis, who had been waiting for that, lured him into an ambush, and of his force only 400 escaped to the Dogra camp. The situation of the Dogra army on the right bank grew worse and worse, as hardly any provisions could be transported there, and the cold of the winter made itself badly felt in the narrow valleys and gorges. It was Basti Ram's energy which saved them. When the despair of the Dogras was at its height, Basti Ram went along the Indus reconnoitring, to see if he could not find a place on the river where the slower current had permitted the formation of an ice-bridge. But such a bridge he could not find. He had, however, several Dards from Da with him, and when they understood what he was in want of they said that they would make him a bridge across the river within a few hours. The Dards make bridges across the Indus in places where they wish to have them every year in winter. Their method is the following: They fasten several beams to the bank in such a way that they project into the river. After a short time they are frozen in an encrustation of ice of such solidity that it is possible to walk on them as far as the outer end. Then several more beams are fastened to the first, and are made to project farther into the river. When they are frozen in, another set of beams is brought, and so on, until the other bank is reached. Such a bridge of ice and wood was built by the Dards, and when it was ready the Dogra army crossed the river at night and surprised the camp of the Baltis, who had not even posted sentinels to warn them. In this night-combat the Baltis were defeated and fled towards Skardo. The castle of Skardo was beleaguered by the united Dogra and Ladakhi armies, and had to surrender soon for want of water. Then Muhamad Shah was made chief of Baltistan, and a fort was built, in which a Dogra garrison was placed.

To warn the Baltis against future revolutions, Zorawar gave them an object lesson at Skardo, showing them what their punishment would be in such a case. Among the Ladakhis who had joined Sukamir in the revolt against the Dogras, there was a certain Rahim Khan, of Chigtan, and a man called Hussein, of Pashkyum. And when the chief of Skardo, Ahmed Shah, had been made prisoner by Zorawar, the latter gave him orders to seize Rahim Khan and bring him to Skardo. Ahmed Shah did not like this kind of business, and tried to avoid it.

But Zorawar threatened him in such a way that he ordered his Baltis to find Rahim Khan, and bring him bound before the Wazir. When both he and Hussein were secured, Zorawar issued an order to all the Dogras, Ladakhis, and Baltis who were assembled at Skardo, to come together in a lucerne field, in the middle of the town. Everybody had to appear, even the women, the old, the lame, and the blind, as Tsebstan tells us. Zorawar and old King Tsepal had a tent erected for each of them. Old Tsepal was to see how those of his subjects were treated who had risked their lives in his cause.

Then Rahim Khan was escorted into the middle of the assembly and placed, bound, before the two tents. There he was told to eat a quantity of hemp, because he was assured it would save him much pain. Butter was again boiled, which made people anticipate what was to happen. Then the executioner appeared and cut off Rahim Khan's right hand, his tongue, his nose, his ears, all the time making ample use of the hot butter, and, having finished, threw his victim in the middle of the crowd. After Rahim Khan, Hussein was treated in a similar way, but he was deprived only of his hand and tongue. He remained alive, whilst Rahim Khan died after two days.

Thus Zorawar had proved once more that he was a genuine Oriental in the treatment of his captives. Still, it must be acknowledged that in this case he was satisfied with torturing two men only, and also that such cases as the execution of the two hundred prisoners at Suru, of which we heard before, were rare occurrences. All the treasures were taken out of the castle of Skardo and carried to Leh, together with Ahmed Shah, the former owner of them.

King Tsepal, General Bangkapa, and the army of Ladakh received permission to return home. However, King Tsepal did not get very far. He had suffered more than his constitution could stand. He was seized with smallpox, and died on the road. Bangkapa met with the same fate. Their corpses were carried to Stog, and there they were burnt.

Now we might imagine that the dynasty had come to an end, but it was not so. Some time before Prince Chogsprul had fled and died, a son was born to him, whose name was Jigsmed namgyal. He was now a boy of eight or nine years, and was acknowledged vassal-king of Ladakh by Zorawar. The Ladakhi chronicles speak of the reign of Ngorub Standzin as having lasted four years. This it is hardly possible to reconcile with the Dogra account. But it may be that during the time of the minority of Jigsmed namgyal, Ngorub Standzin was restored to grace and made regent.

Although the reign of Jigsmed namgyal was extremely short, as we shall see, people sing a song in praise of it. It is as follows :—

If a castle ought to be called high, it is the castle Skukar.
If a palace ought to be called high, it is the palace of Leh.
On this height sits the Lord of All.
On this summit of happiness sits Jigsmed namgyal.
As the four continents are filled with light,
The earth is filled with grain.

The good omens are fulfilled,
The sun of happiness is risen.
All the inhabitants of the strong castle are like a knot in their devotion to religious custom.

This knot and the good omens are only one.
The joyful omens are fulfilled;
The sun of happiness is risen.

14

The War Against Central Tibet, 1841-1842

AFTER the Balti war Zorawar did not go to Jammu, but remained in Ladakh, and made preparations for another great expedition into Central Asia. The main reason for his new plan was probably to give employment to his master's many new subjects in Ladakh and Baltistan, and in this way to keep their thoughts from revolutionary ideas. Besides, he seems gradually to have discovered that he was a genius in conquering, and that his gift had to be given a new field of activity. He spoke of conquering Yarkand and Central Asia in general. That he started first of all on the conquest of Rutog, Guge, and Purang was probably due to his studies in Western Tibetan history. He seems to have been told that in its best times the Western Tibetan empire comprised those now Central Tibetan provinces, and the Dogras, as the present masters of Western Tibet, revived the claims to those outlying districts.

It was a great mistake on the part of Zorawar to start on this new expedition at the approach of winter. He had probably forgotten entirely what difficulties the winter campaign in 1834 had brought him. Or had Zorawar a particular liking for winter campaigns? In this case it was absolute folly to lead an Indian army in winter to a battle-field which was situated at an altitude of 15,000 feet. What the cold in those regions may be like in December can be imagined when I state that, when once spending a night in a tent in those altitudes in June, the contents of a teapot became one lump of ice before morning. However, Zorawar seems to have lulled himself into such a certainty of victory that difficulties were no more worthy of consideration.

The army was comprised of Baltis, Ladakhis, and 6000-7000 Dogras. Of the Ladakhis the greater part had to do transport work. Each peasant was made responsible for 240 pounds, which load he had to convey on horses, yaks, donkeys, or on his own back.

It was a long time before the Dogra army was met by a Tibetan force. After having passed the frontier the first places worth noticing were the great monasteries of Hanle and Trashisgang, which were plundered. Their treasures were conveyed to Leh. Basti Ram was sent in advance to Dagla kar (Taklakar) in Purang, the fort of which place he held with a garrison of about five hundred men. A Mohammedan of Chushod, near Leh, Rahim Khan, was placed over Spiti, and this man's son-in-law, Ghulam Khan, made himself useful as iconoclast. Idol-breaking appeared to be the most congenial occupation Ghulam khan had ever engaged in, and soon he could boast of having cleared Spiti of all its images.

The vanguard of Zorawar's army was a Ladakhi corps, under the leadership of a certain Nono Sodnam. He was sent to oppose the approaching Tibetan army with three hundred men. This force was found quite insufficient, and therefore he was sent once more with six hundred men. When he met the Tibetan army the second time, he had Ghulam khan, the iconoclast, with him. They were hopelessly beaten, and their force annihilated. Nono Sodnam and Ghulam khan were made prisoners.

The bulk of the Dogra army was concentrated at Tirtapur, between Gartog and Daglakar. It advanced from Tirtapur in an easterly direction, probably in order to get into touch with Basti Ram's detachment at Daglakar. The Tibetan army was met on the 10th December, on a plain, about 15,000 feet above sea-level. The cold was intense, and when during the night much snow and hail fell, the Dogras suffered severely, and some whose clothing was quite insufficient died. Zorawar threw up trenches, and about these there was a three day's combat. On the 12th December. Zorawar received a bullet in his right shoulder. He was, however, not ready to give in at once, and seized his sword with his left hand. But the Tibetans knew very well that the Dogra leader was wounded. They made a desperate rush on the trenches, and a Tibetan horseman thrust his lance through Zorawar's breast. This put an end to his life and to the resistance of his army. Once the Dogras had given way, the whole army was seized with a panic and fled in a disorderly manner. All the principal officers and many men were captured. Many others died from cold in the flight; and of the whole army only about one thousand reached Leh alive. The garrison of Daglakar fled, and the provinces of Purang, Guge, and Rutog were soon in the hands of the Tibetans.

The many prisoners, Ladakhis as well as Dogras, were transported to Lhasa, where they were treated variously, but on the whole kindly. Thus, the ex-chief of Baltistan, Ahmed Shah, who, with his favourite second son, spent his last days in Lhasa, was even treated with courtesy and respect. The fate of one prisoner only was deplorable, that of Ghulam khan, the talented iconoclast. His treatment of the monasteries could not be passed by without a lesson, and he was slowly tortured to death with hot irons.

Now that the greatest general the Dogras have ever had has found his death on the battle-field, let us pause for a moment and place a wreath of tribute on his grave. For, Oriental though he was, we cannot help admiring a greatness in this man by which he by far surpassed his surroundings. In the beginning of his conquests he was extremely cautious; but this was essentially necessary, considering the naturally protected position of Western Tibet, and his entire want of knowledge of the geographical conditions of this country. But, as he had a keen eye for the defects of his enemy, and was a great strategist, all these difficulties were overcome. After the conquest was completed, the continual insurrections presented a new problem for his ingenuity to solve. By the manner in which he treated them, and in which he quelled them one after another, without any extra amount of cruelty, he showed not a little measure of wisdom. He proved himself a true soldier in the endurance of extraordinary hardships, and in setting an example of personal courage; and if he had not met with an early end on the battle-field, he might have impressed his name on the pages of the great history of the world.

The disastrous end of the Dogra campaign against Central

Tibet had a result similar to Napoleon's retreat from Moscow. The hope of the Ladakhis of regaining their independence was revived once more, and from all parts of the country, even from Baltistan, matchlock-men arrived, and the two forts of Leh, which held a Dogra garrison of about 350 men, were blockaded. The number of the Ladakhi warriors who acknowledged the boy-king, Jigsmed namgyal, as their only sovereign, was 2500, according to the chronicles. Also detachments of the Central Tibetan army arrived at Leh, to assist the Ladakhis in their struggle for liberty. The principal of these Tibetans was Pishi, the head of the bowmen, who lived in grand style at the Leh palace.

But Jigsmed namgyal's reign was destined only to last six weeks. For soon the news arrived in Ladakh that a fresh Dogra army of 7000 men, under the command of Devan Harichand and Ratun, was advancing to Leh with cannons and excellent equipment. Pishi and the other Tibetans had not come to Leh to be killed there, and they decided on fleeing, taking along with them the boy-king and his ministers. They fled in the direction of the Upper Indus valley, whilst the Ladakhi matchlock-men returned to their own villages. When the Dogras arrived in Leh, they destroyed all the idols they found in the castle and monastery. That was a new procedure, for up to now they had spared all the Buddhist establishments, as they respected in Buddhism an originally Indian form of religion.

The fugitive party had arrived meanwhile at Drangtse, near the western end of the Panggong lake, and there they were joined by a Tibetan army of 3000 men under the command of Ragasha and Zurkang. At Drangtse, the Tibetans dug trenches and erected a fortified camp. Before the Dogras arrived there Zurkang marched against them, attacked them on the plateau of Darkhug, and after he had done some damage to them went back to his fortified camp. This camp was situated in the lower part of a narrow valley, and the storming of it would have meant considerable loss on the side of the Dogras. Therefore the latter decided on driving the Tibetans out of their stronghold by means of a flood. The Dogras dammed up the water in the valley in such a way that the Tibetan trenches were flooded and had to be deserted. Outside their fortifications the Tibetans were not equal to the well-armed Dogras. Most of them fled, and several were made prisoners, among them their general Ragasha. Ragasha was decapitated, for he was a welcome subject to the Dogras to revenge the death of Zorawar on the Tibetans.

Then a peace was concluded with the Tibetans, according to which the annual trade between Lhasa and Leh was reinstituted, the Dogras taking the place and obligations of the Ladakhi kings. Jigsmed namgyal had to be satisfied with the village of Stog and the taxes of its few peasants, and hardly a single one of the old Ladakhi state officials remained in office.

According to Tsebstan, after some time an exchange of prisoners took place between Lhasa and Jammu. He says: "Then the Dogra prisoners returned from Lhasa, each with his Tibetan wife and one child. Also the Tibetan prisoners returned from Jammu, each with an Indian wife and two or three children." Among the Dogra prisoners who returned from Lhasa to Jammu was a certain Reyo Singh, and of him Tsebstan tells the following anecdote: "The Maharaja asked him, 'If once more we go to war against Tibet, shall we win or not?' To which Reyo Singh replied, 'We shall not succeed in gaining a victory over the Tibetans. As many soldiers as we have, so many Lamas have the Tibetans; as much food as a Dogra consumes within a month, a Tibetan eats within a day; as many dresses as are put on by ten Dogras, a single Tibetan puts on. Besides, they have great magicians, who make rain and fire, as they please, who can also cause heaven and earth to shake. Some men come flying down from the sky. Others make themselves invisible, and kill with a sword whom they please; and there is much more which has not its equal in other countries.' The Maharaja did not like this speech, and said, 'You are taking the side of the Tibetans!' and sent him away."

Since then, there has been peace. Only, in 1846 a little rebellion broke out in Zangskar, which was promptly repressed by Basti Ram. Thus Ladakh had become part of the Jammu State, and, after 1846, of the Jammu and Kashmir State, and the blessing of the Pax Britannica has made itself felt in our country also. But another blessing of British rule, the wise administration of revenues, and the encouragement of the much shaken agriculture of the country, have been withheld from Ladakh, as the administration remained in the hands of Dogra and Kashmir officials. Since 1842 the country has made little progress. This is even observed by the natives, who compare other portions of Western Tibet which have come under British rule, in particular Lahoul, with their own country; and the difference between the two districts economically is surprising. As, however, the rulers of the Kashmir State can no longer keep their eyes shut to the example set by British India and a number of progressive Native States, there is hope that more attention will in future be paid to the development of the agriculture of Ladakh, and perhaps the standard of happiness which was attained under some of the best native Tibetan rulers will once more be reached.

The Ladakhis sing a song of Zorawar's wife, whom they believe to have accompanied her husband to Ladakh, and who had to return alone across the Zoji Pass. In this song Urdu words are mixed in a quaint way with the Tibetan.

I do not wish to eat bread received from the sinful northerners:
I do not wish to drink water received from the sinful northerners.
Amidst the inhabitants of this land I have no friends and relations;
In the northern plain I have no brothers and friends.
In the place of friends and relations I had only Zorawar.
In the place of brothers and friends I had only Zorawar.
And it was only Zorawar who made me a despised widow.
And it was only Zorawar who made his queen a despised widow
When arriving on the Zoji Pass, my fatherland can be seen.
When arriving on the Zoji Pass, Lahore and the Panjab can be seen.
Although I can see my fatherland, I shall not arrive there.
Although I can see my fatherland, Zorawar's queen will not arrive there.

15

Missionary's Review

Now that the historian has done his work, let the missionary add a few words. I hope that all those who have any judgment in the matter will acknowledge that in the preceding pages it has been my endeavour to give an objective picture of the history of Western Tibet, as true as is possible in the present state of historical research. As, however, my position as a missionary gives my interest in the country a very subjective colouring, I wish to discuss a few questions from a missionary point of view.

The present age is an age not only of world politics but also of world religion. The great and the minor religions of almost every nation meet with general interest. But hardly any of them is studied with more fervour than Buddhism. Occasionally even the Christian nations are admonished to express their gratitude for one or the other blessing which, as they are told, has its roots in Buddhism. Buddhism claims to be a religion of peace and goodwill towards all creatures, and with regard to this a passage from Koppen's *Lamaistische Hierarchie* has been quoted in a great number of books. Koppen points to the fact that the Mongolians, who in former ages used to be the terror of Europe, have left the European continent undisturbed since the battle of Liegnitz, 1241, or, roughly speaking, since the time they adopted Lamaism. This continual danger to Europe was averted, we are told, not by the energy of European arms, but by the instilling of a religion of peace in this warlike nation. This kind of argument can only be used with success before a public which has not the slightest knowledge of the history of the Mongols. And the present history of the Western Tibetans does not speak of a continual area of peace in their own territories either. Neither the Mongolians nor the Tibetans have become any more peaceful by the adoption of Lamaism than they were before. That they did not carry their expeditions as far as Europe can be explained by the fact that they were kept busy nearer home. The Chinese and the Turks had to be fought first, and internal wars hardly ever ceased.

It would be surprising, indeed, if the Buddhist doctrine of peace had met with general acceptance, considering the lax attitude of the population towards other Buddhist precepts. Buddhism would never have spread over the greater part of Asia if it had insisted on a strict observance of its doctrines. It was quite satisfied to be formally ackowledged as the religion of a country, and left the morals and customs of the laity of the nation in their former condition. It may be said that also on the occasion of the introduction of Christianity into various European countries, concessions were made to the ancient religions of those countries. Quite true, but Christianity was not content to be thus formally acknowledged only, but proved itself a transforming power, which by and by penetrated the entire life of the nations. One of the ugliest customs, morally, of Tibet is the system of polyandry. It was certainly not introduced by Buddhism, but Buddhism has never raised a finger against it. Before its abolition, there is no hope that the moral condition of the Tibetans can be raised. As the history shows us, the kings who could afford to be polygamists indulged in this custom too. There are European scientists, among them Ramsay, late British Joint Commissioner to Ladakh, who vindicate the custom of polyandry with regard to Tibet. Desert as the country is, they say it can give sustenance only to a very limited number of inhabitants. To prevent the population from increasing, this system was invented, and it would be a misfortune if, with the introduction of Christianity, monogamy was introduced. These philosophers, Ramsay among them, entirely forget that, before the introduction of Christianity, Mohammedanism had entered the country, and that, together with it, polygamy began to spread The supposed aim of polyandry, to keep the population within narrow limits, can only be reached if a number of women are ready to remain single. Spinsters, however, are hardly found in non-Christian countries. At the present time those women who are not married by Lamaists find it easy to become the wives of the many Mohammedan merchants at Leh, although they are often married for a very short period only to a certain man. Instead of assailing Christianity, our wise philosophers had better attack Mohammedanism as a harmful system. Still, in spite of Mohammedanism and the beginning of Christianity, the country (Ladakh proper) is far from being overpopulated. Immorality, nurtured by polyandry, has so undermined the powers of increase of the people that uncared-for orphan children are almost non-existent. Orphan children are adopted at the first opportunity, because most of the peasants are short of hands to work their fields properly.

But we must not forget that the inhabitants of Western Tibet have to be grateful to Buddhism for one important acquisition, the art of reading and writing. Long before the commencement of Lamaism, in the first centuries before Christ, the Indian Brahmi alphabet, used for Sanskrit, entered the deserts of Western Tibet as the first script. It was followed by several other Indian scripts, specimens of which have been found, dating from the beginning of our era down to the eleventh century. These scripts are: Kharoshthi, of the Kushana era; Brahmi, of the Kushana era; Indian characters, of the eighth or ninth and of the eleventh century. The most important alphabet was the Tibetan alphabet, which in its present form may have been introduced during the eighth or ninth century. Its importance rests on the fact that Tibetan conquered the territories of the Dard and Mon languages, and was the vehicle of a vast literature. At first this literature must have exercised a certain influence on those who studied it. But as the aims of its study were not enlightenment but the accumulation of religious merit, the influence of its doctrines became less and less. It became petrified, and the reading of it degenerated into a rattling off of syllables, the meaning of which was not considered worthy of reflection.

Suddenly Western Tibet was overrun by Mohammedans, the most western portions were entirely converted to

Mohammedanism, whilst the capital and its surroundings received a considerable sprinkling of the new religion. Therefore the question is not without interest: Has the new religion proved to have any elevating powers, as compared with Lamaism? In savage countries, Mohammedanism has certainly been the means of elevating people to a higher standard than they had before its arrival. It is different in countries which possess a culture of their own. Thus, in Western Tibet I find it impossible to discover any progress which can be put to the credit of the Mohammedans. I will not say that the country has deteriorated. It seems to have remained much the same. The art of reading and writing, as possessed by the Ladakhis and Baltis, was not acknowledged by the Mohammedans, in whose eyes only a knowledge of the Arabic characters was of any value. So, in the Mussulman territories this new alphabet and the reading of the Koran in Arabic were taught. As also in this case the understanding of the religious text was considered to be of minor importance, the general education of the people remained on the same low level it had reached before. Still, one doctrine of Mohammedanism attained popularity and influence amongst its adherents: the doctrine of One God Only, and of the vanity of all idols. This is the great truth and strength of this religion, and on account of it Mohammedanism spreads also in those lands where it is not supported by arms. This doctrine appeals to the common sense of all nations, as do the Ten Commandments; and the vanity of the modern Hindo saying, "People must be led to a higher understanding of God by beginning with visible representations of Him!" is proved by the quick and general acceptance of the Moslem truth. But, unfortunately, the understanding of this great truth, which is not connected with a moral system of high standard, makes its adherents self-contented and conceited, especially if they are surrounded by idolaters. Mussulmans are always in danger of developing into Pharisees, and mission work among them is as difficult now as Christ found it to be among the Pharisees.

But mission work among Buddhists and Lamaists is not very easy either. A Buddhist Lama who has understood the doctrines of his system to a certain degree looks down with contempt on every other wisdom, and is quite capable of enveloping himself in as much conceit as the ordinary Mussulman does. The laity, who have to be satisfied with the grossest idolatry, are kept in strict dependence on the ecclesiastical institutions; for the monasteries have developed into a sort of banking establishments, and there is hardly a peasant who is not in debt to one or the other monastery.

Does it not look like a hopeless enterprise to do mission work in a country where Lamaism and Mohammedanism meet? And yet, God, who claims to be also the God of the heathen, as the prophets of the Old Testament assert, claims also the steppes of Western Tibet as His own. That He is the God of the heathen He has proved, as I believe, also in the history of Western Tibet. As was noted above, even the heathen Ladakhis believe they can see His hand in the story of blind King Lhawang namgyal, who was dethroned by his brother Trashi namgyal. When hearing that Trashi remained without children, they exclaim: "How just is God" although, according to Buddhist philosophy, they ought to be pure atheists. And we can well imagine that a king who, like Bum lde, tried his best to fulfil the precepts of his religion, imperfect though it was, is more graciously looked upon by the God of the heathen than many another whose thoughts never rose above the things of this world. But when looking at the inroads of Mohammedanism and the unhappy fate of the kingdom during its last decades, we cannot help recognising the hand of our God, who prepared the country for the coming of Christianity. This preparation took place according to a similar method, though on a smaller scale, as occurred in Europe before the advent of Christ.

Hard to conquer though both are, Mohammedanism as well as Buddhism, they were both weakened by being brought in contact with each other. This can be plainly observed in Leh. The adherents of both religions are most bigoted in those territories where they never get to see adherents of other creeds. In a religiously mixed population the belief in the infallibility of any particular religion is often shaken, and in consequence of this the religious convictions of any one creed become weaker. Although the next result of such a process is indifference towards any form of religion, still, in a soil of that kind,

Christianity is more acceptable than it was before the process began. The indifference towards religion is particularly exemplified in the case of marriages at Leh. The girls generally change their religion like a dress. They become Buddhists if they have an opportunity to marry a Buddhist husband, and Mohammedans in the other case.

The hand of God showed its power in particular during the last decades of the Western Tibetan empire, when it was against it. Of the last two brother-kings, Tsestan died as a young man. He was superior as a ruler to many of his predecessors, and might have been the man to strengthen his kingdom to such an extent as to be able to resist the Dogras. And during the Dogra war the only leader who might have carried the war to a glorious end, the young minister of Stog, lost his life in one of the first battles. It is quite evident the time had arrived for the kingdom to come to an end, and it could not be saved by men. It was to become impregnated with the great flood of new conceptions and ideas which had found their way to India, and, together with them, the great problem of Christian missions was to be realised in Western Tibet. The progress of the mission work was slow in the beginning, but has become a little quicker in course of time, and the importance of this work for the Christianisation of the whole of Tibet cannot be overestimated. Here, not only the methods for the evangelisation of Tibet proper can be learned, but the fact is demonstrated to the Tibetans that it is quite possible to be a Tibetan by birth and yet a Christian by re-birth. God grant that in no very far future the history of Tibet may enter upon a new phase, that of a Christian Tibet!

Appendices

APPENDIX I

Rinchana Bhoti's Career, According to Material Supplied by Dr J. Ph. Vogel

THE Tibetan record does not contain more than Prince Rinchen's name, but the chronicles of Kashmir have a long chapter on a Tibetan prince Rinchana, who was king of Kashmir about 1319-1323 A.D., and it is quite probable that the two are identical, although it is somewhat difficult to reconcile the Kashmir record with what we know of West Tibetan history. According to the Kashmir chronicles, it was the murder of Rinchana's father, *Vakatanya*, by a tribe of *Kalamanyas*, that caused Rinchana's departure from Tibet. The word *Kalamanya* probably stands for "men of Kharmang", Kharmang being the capital of a tribe of Baltis; and it looks almost as if the Baltis had at that time tried to annihilate the Ladakhi dynasty. The name *Vakatanya* may refer to the castle of *Vaka* near Mulbe, which was in the hands of the Ladakhi kings. We shall hardly ever get beyond the realm of supposition with regard to the political state of Western Tibet of those days, and must not expect the Kashmir chronicler to have troubled much about Rinchana's early history. There are three reasons in particular which make us believe in the possible identity of *rGyalbu rinchen* and the *Rinchana* of Kashmir: (1) the fact that the Tibetan record speaks of *Rinchen* only as a "prince" (*rgyalbu*); (2) the identity of name; (3) the approximate identity of time. Still, I do not consider the proof sufficient enough to compel me to alter my system of chronology in favour of the Kashmir date 1319-1329.

But even if Rinchana could be proved to be of Balti or Purig instead of Ladakhi descent, a history of Western Tibet would not be complete without mentioning him.

After having avenged his family on the people of *Kalamanya*, Rinchana proceeded to Kashmir. He arrived there at a time of great disorder, which had been caused by the raid of a Turkish invader called *Druluca*. The king of Kashmir, *Suhadeva*, was a good-for-nothing man. But the minister of Kashmir, *Ramachandra*, took up arms against the Turks. When he was murdered by the Tibetans, and *Druluca* sent out of the country, Rinchana became undisputed master of the country and married Queen Kota, the wife or daughter of Ramachandra.

Order was at once restored, and the Kashmir chronicles praise the time of Rinchana's government in the highest terms. To illustrate his wisdom in pronouncing judgment, two Solomon-like stories are told:—

Two mares, which grazed in the same forest, had each a colt. A lion killed one of the colts, and the owners of the mares both claimed the surviving colt as their own. King Rinchana ordered the two mares and the colt to be brought on board a ship on the river Jhelum, and when the middle of the current was reached he threw the colt overboard. At once the mare which was the real mother jumped into the water after the colt, whilst the other one only neighed.

The other story runs as follows: One of Rinchana's followers was reported to have taken milk from a cowherd without payment. The man denied having taken any. In order to ascertain the truth, Rinchana ordered the man's stomach to be cut open. When the milk gushed forth Rinchana's wisdom was greatly admired; but one wonders how he would have mended his mistake if the victim had not been guilty!

Later on, some of Rinchana's Tibetan followers, at the instigation of the Turk Druluca, made an attempt to murder the king. They were headed by Tulkka (probably *Drugpa* in Tibetan), but were not successful. However, Rinchana died a few months after from headache, caused by a cold.

The son who was born to him in Kashmir did not succeed him as king of Kashmir. But, before leaving Ladakh, rGyalbu

Rinchen apparently had a son who became king of Ladakh, for there is no break in the line of Ladakhi kings.

APPENDIX II

The Ancient History of Lahoul

THE ancient, history of Lahoul differs from that of Ladakh. It is contained chiefly in the languages of the country. The fact that the little country of Lahoul possesses three distinct languages which are not related to the Aryan languages of India, and only distantly related to Tibetan, has long been a puzzle to philologists. The grand work of the Linguistic Survey of India, recently undertaken by the Indian Government, has, however, done much towards elucidating the problem of Lahoul among many others.

The excellent material which the Rev. J. Bruske, one of the Moravian missionaries, prepared for the Linguistic Survey revealed the fact that the grammar of the Kanaweri language, which is spoken in the neighbourhood of Chini, on the Sutlej, has strong affinities to the languages of the Mundaris, who live to the south-west of Calcutta. As the Kanaweri language was known to be closely related to the three languages of Lahoul, these languages, Bunan, Manchat, and Tinan, were examined in search of similar affinities, and it was proved that their relationship to the Mundari languages was exactly the same as that of Kanaweri.

As regards their vocabulary, the three languages of Lahoul show a strong resemblance to Tibetan; but, as regards their grammar, they differ widely from any Tibetan dialect, and show surprising coincidences with Mundari.

Let us first examine the Mundari side of the question. To a Tibetan student of the three languages of Lahoul the following facts appear extraordinary : (1) Higher numbers are counted in twenties instead of in tens. Thus fifty is "twice twenty and ten" (*nyis sai chui*) in Bunan. (2) The complicated system of personal pronouns. All these languages have not only double forms for "we," one including the person addressed, and the other excluding the same (one corresponding to the English "I and you," the other to the English "I and they"), as also many Tibetan dialects have it; but they possess also dual and plural forms of the pronouns. Thus, before selecting the proper word for "we," "our," "us," etc., in these languages, the speaker has to think as follows: Are there two or more persons who make up the "we"? Do I include the person or persons before me in the "we," or do I not? Reason enough to cause a beginner in these languages to hesitate before he pronounces the word "we"! (3) The three languages of Lahoul have very full systems of conjugation, with terminations for the different persons, singular and plural, whilst the Tibetan verb hardly ever distinguishes between persons. Thus "I made, thou madest," etc., is conjugated in Bunan and Tibetan in the following way:—

Bunan.	*Tibetan.*
ligkiza	chospin
ligzana	chospin
ligza	chospin
liitsa	chospin
ligtsani	chospin
ligtsa	chospin

(4) The three languages of Lahoul have a very strange system of pronominal "interfix," so to speak, *i.e.*, the incorporation of the object in the verb. As we have seen, *ligza* means in Bunan "he made." A word to express "for me," or "me," is *ku*. If I wish to say "he made for me," I have to divide the word *ligza* and insert the word *ku* between its two parts. Thus *ligkuza*, "he made for me." (5) The three languages of Lahoul contain a certain class of sounds which is entirely foreign to the Tibetan system of phonetics. They are the half-pronounced *g* and *d* sounds, which occur at the end of words. Their sound is almost as comical and extraordinary to the European

fruits, and on raw flesh : and they knew neither the breeding of cattle nor the tilling of the land, nor had they any settled laws or forms of government. They made pots of clay, and baked them in the fire. They buried their dead, and over their graves they set up upright slabs of rock or circles of stone. It is from these, and the things found in them, that we are able to form some idea of the life and customs of the wild aborigines."

The Tibetan element of their parentage is represented more particularly in the vocabulary of the three languages of Lahoul; and, indeed, these languages have preserved to the present day a number of Tibetan words in a more archaic form than can be found in any Tibetan dialect or archaeological document Such a word is the word *gyag* ([*r*]*gyag*), "day," Tibetan *zhag*. We know from Tibetan dialects that *gy* can become *j*, and *j* is often changed into *zh*. In all Tibetan records the word for "day" is *zhag*, and it is only from Lahouli that we learn that in very remote times it was probably pronounced *gyag*. Another example is the word for "life," *shrog* in Tibetan and *strog* in Lahouli. Tibetan phonetics teach us that the pronunciation *str*, *skr*, etc., preceded the present pronunciation *shr*. But this word is represented in its ancient form in none of the most archaic Tibetan documents, and we know only from Lahouli that the word *shrog* was actually preceded by an ancient word *strog*. As regards the Tibetan vowel system, we know that *a* is a more original vowel than *o*, if it occurs in the same root. Thus we can imagine that several words which contain an *o* at the present time may have had an *a* in earlier days. Now we find a number of Tibetan words which contain an *a* only in Lahouli; for instance, *tang* or *thang*, "see," Tibetan *thong*; *lag*, "return," Tibetan *log*, etc. Thus, also in this case, the languages of Lahoul have preserved a state of things which preceded by a long way even the most archaic type of Tibetan known.

Thus the Tibetan side of the question comes in to confirm what has to be surmised from the Mundari evidence, viz., that the amalgamation of the two peoples must have taken place at a very early date, probably before the immigration of the Aryans into India. But something more should be said regarding the Tibetan element in the languages of Lahoul, in particular Bunan. Besides the pre-classical Tibetan words found in Bunan, as mentioned above, we have traces of yet a second and a third flood of Tibetan words which have entered this language. The second flood is represented by Tibetan words the pronunciation of which is in harmony with the ancient classical orthography of Tibetan, whilst in modern Tibetan the pronunciation has become different from the original spelling. This influx of Tibetan words into Bunan is best illustrated by an extract from the Rev. H. A. Jaschke's list :—

Bunan.	*Tibetan* (classial orthography).	*Tibetan* (modern pronunciation).
Khral	Khral	ṭhal
Grogpo	Grogpo	ḍogpo
Phyugpo	Phyugpo	chugpo
Bri	Bri	ḍi
Brang	Brang	ḍang

This list of words testifies to the great influence which the Tibetans must have exercised in the Bunan valley, say, about the days of Christ, when their pronunciation may have been in accordance with the present classical spelling.

The third influx of Tibetan is represented by another group of Tibetan loan-words in Bunan, the pronunciation of which is not in accordance with the classical Tibetan orthography but with the present Tibetan pronunciation. The following are a few specimens taken from Jaschke's list :—

Bunan.	*Tibetan* (classical orthography).	*Tibetan* (modern pronunciation).
ṭam	kram	tam
ṭhim	khrims	ṭhim
jungva	byungba	jungva
chodpa	spyodpa	chodpa
ḍoi	gros	ḍoi

This last influx of Tibetan words must have taken place in historical times —

In the same manner as Bunan was influenced by Tibetan, the other two languages of Lahoul (Manchat and Tinan) were influenced later on by Aryan Indian languages; for the neighbouring States of Kulu and Chamba were conquered by Aryan tribes, the intercourse with whom brought the introduction of many Aryan loan-words.

As with the languages, so it is with the religious customs of Lahoul. They also represent a very mixed state of things. There is a certain ancient custom which is observed nowadays only in Manchat, and which probably goes back to old Mundari times. It is the custom of putting up a slab of stone by the roadside in commemoration of a deceased person. These may be seen near every village in Manchat. Those erected more recently have a spot smeared with oil in the middle. Many of the stones are quite plain, but there are some which have a rock-carving representing a human figure in the centre, and others again have a sculpture representing the deceased person, in relief. The last phase in the development of the originally plain commemorative stones is found in the village temples. There we see large slabs of stone on which are carved often more than ten persons in a row. They are well bathed in oil. On making my special inquiry, the natives told me that at irregular periods all the rich families who had lost a member through death had to combine and give a great feast to the whole village. In recognition of this, a slab containing the never-flattering portraits of the dead is placed in the village temple. The more ancient of these slabs are of a certain anthropological interest, as they represent the people of Lahoul in their original costume. In the olden days people wore nothing but a little frock, reaching from the loins to the knees, and the chiefs (apparently) had a head-dress of feathers, similar to that of the North American Indians This kind of dress we find represented on very old commemorative slabs at Triloknath, and on a rock-carving of a man hunting wild sheep near Kyelang. The wild sheep (*Shapo*) has been extinct in Lahoul for many centuries, and it is only through this rock-carving that we know of its former existence in Lahoul.

The most ancient religion of Lahoul was probably *phallus* and snake worship—the two representing the creative powers of the sun and water. As regards the phallus worship, we have to distinguish between the original custom, which was satisfied with a raw stone of phallus-shape put up in a little grove or beside the door of a village temple, and the modern Hindu custom. The former is still the most common form of phallus worship in the country. But in Manchat there may also be seen a few well-polished phallus stones, which were introduced when the modern form of Hinduism gained some ground in the country. The upper end of the ancient phallus stones is smeared with oil or butter, whilst the modern ones are sprinkled with water, as in India. The village temples are small huts with a sloping gable roof of shingles, and have a ram's head, the symbol of the creative power, carved at the end of the uppermost beam of the roof. In these huts the most ancient form of habitation of the Lahoulis is still preserved. The peasants have meanwhile taken to the Tibetan type of house, with flat roofs consisting of willow branches and earth, probably because this kind of material can be obtained more readily.

In a country where phallus worship is the rule, we can imagine that by the side of great licentiousness cruel customs are in vogue. And, indeed, popular tradition all over the country speaks of human sacrifices which were offered in order to ensure a good harvest. The custom reminds us strongly of that prevailing until quite recently among the Khonds of India. At Kyelang the following story is told with regard to the last human sacrifice : A man had to be killed every year for the benefit of the fields of the community. The peasants were to offer the victim in turns. (They probably kept slaves, and *these* were generally killed.) One year it was a poor widow's turn, and as she had no servants, it was understood that her only son was to be sacrificed. Whilst she was weeping sadly about this, a wandering hermit came to her house and offered to die in the place of her son, if she would feed him well until the day of execution. The widow gladly accepted the offer, and on the appointed day the hermit was led with much noise before the wooden idol of the god of the fields. When the executioner walked up with his axe to the hermit, the latter said : "Wait a little, dear friend : lend me your axe, and let me see if the god really wants to take my life." Then he stepped with the axe before the idol and said, "Well, Lord of the Fields, if you really want my life, take it please; if not, I shall take yours." As there was no reply, the hermit raised his axe and cut the idol in pieces. Then he threw the fragments into the river, and everybody went home. The water carried the fragments as far as the village of Gugti, where they were caught and put up again.[1] The consequence of the hermit's Bonifacius-like deed was, that, ever since, the local deity had to be satisfied with the sacrifice of a goat; and people say that their deity still becomes frightened if the name of the courageous Lama is pronounced in his presence.

In Manchat, human sacrifices were not offered with the same regularity as at Kyelang, but apparently only in cases of dearth. The last victim, according to local tradition, was the queen *Rupi rani*. She was buried alive against her will, and her last words were a curse upon the land. She prayed that henceforth the inhabitants of the land should not grow older than she was on the day of her death, and people believe that this curse is still being fulfilled. In provinces bordering on Lahoul —for instance, in Kangra—the human sacrifices continued in a milder form down to the nineteenth century. The victim was forced to perform some dangerous task or other. If he got through it alive, it was understood that the local deity was willing to exist without a taste of human blood for another year.

Buddhism seems to have entered Lahoul from India in the eighth century A.D. We suppose this to have happened, because the name of *Padma sambhava*, the famous Buddhist missionary of that time, is mentioned, not only in connection with the most ancient Buddhist monasteries of Lahoul, but even in connection with Hindu places of worship in the adjoining provinces. It is of some interest that in the ancient book called *Padma bka btang* the countries Zahor (Tibetan for Mandi) and Gazha (=Garzha) are mentioned among the countries visited by *Padma sambhava* ; and even the name Gandola occurs among those of the monasteries founded by the same Lama.

1. According to another version the god of the fields lived in a rose tree, which was carried to Gugti by the water and there planted again.

These ancient Buddhist temples are wooden structures with pyramidal roofs, and exhibit interesting ancient wood-carvings. Three are known : the Gandola monastery, at the confluence of the Chandra and Bhaga Rivers ; the Kangani monastery, in Manchat; and Triloknath. Kangani even has traces of pictures painted in blue and reddish-brown colours alone, which are otherwise found only in sites of very ancient Buddhist art in Ladakh and Yarkand.

When the history of Lahoul became bound up with the history of the West Tibetan empire,[1] Buddhism entered the country once more in the form of Lamaism, whose many monasteries are distinguished by their flat roofs. At the same time, from the Chamba side the influence of Aryan Hinduism made itself felt. As archaeology shows, this happened during the reign of the Chamba kings Jasata and Lalitavurman in the 11th century. The latter brought the people the modern phallic emblem (*lingam*), and taught them the more refined art of stone sculpture, with which they have thereafter decorated their walls.

But whether the Lahoulis inclined more towards Lamaism or towards Hinduism, Triloknath remained their favourite place of pilgrimage. The following is one of the prayers which are sung on the way to Triloknath (*Lad. Songs*, No. XLVI.):—

O, exalted one !
Give us a child; O may it be granted !
Mayest thou show us mercy !
We shall offer three a great sacrifice,
O exalted one !

1. Lahoul was in a loose way part of the Ladhaki empire from about 1150 to 1647 A.D.; then it became part of the kingdom of Kulu.

INDEX